# The Up & Running Series from SYBEX

. . . . . . . . . .

Other titles include Up & Running with:

- **AutoSketch 3**
- **Carbon Copy Plus**
- **DOS 3.3**
- **Flight Simulator**
- **Harvard Graphics**
- **Lotus 1-2-3 Release 2.2**
- **Lotus 1-2-3 Release 3.1**
- **Norton Utilities**
- **PageMaker 4 on the PC**
- **PageMaker on the Macintosh**
- **PC Tools Deluxe 6**
- **PC-Write**
- **PROCOMM PLUS**
- **Q & A**
- **Quattro Pro 3**
- **Quicken 4**
- **ToolBook for Windows**
- **Turbo Pascal 5.5**
- **Windows 3.0**
- **Windows 286/386**
- **WordPerfect Library/Office PC**
- **XTreeGold 2**
- **Your Hard Disk**

# Up & Running with Norton Utilities® 5

Michael Gross

SYBEX ®

San Francisco ■ Paris ■ Düsseldorf ■ Soest

Acquisitions Editor: Dianne King
Series Editor: Joanne Cuthbertson
Copy Editor: Brendan Fletcher
Technical Editor: Joseph C. Liburt
Word Processors: Scott Campbell, Ann Dunn, Lisa Mitchell, Susan Trybull
Series Designers: Ingrid Owen, Helen Bruno
Icon Designer: Helen Bruno
Screen Graphics: Cuong Le
Desktop Production Specialist: Deborah Maizels
Pasteup: Suzanne Albertson
Proofreader: Lisa Haden
Indexer: Tom McFadden
Cover Designer: Archer Design
Some screen reproductions produced by XenoFont.

XenoFont is a trademark of XenoSoft.

SYBEX is a registered trademark of SYBEX, Inc.

TRADEMARKS: SYBEX has attempted throughout this book to distinguish propri-
etary trademarks from descriptive terms by following the capitalization style used by
the manufacturer.

SYBEX is not affiliated with any manufacturer.

Every effort has been made to supply complete and accurate information. However,
SYBEX assumes no responsibility for its use, nor for any infringement of the intel-
lectual property rights of third parties which would result from such use.

Library of Congress Card Number: 91-65089
ISBN: 0-89588-819-X

Manufactured in the United States of America
10 9 8 7 6 5 4 3 2 1

■ ■ ■ ■ ■ ■ ■ ■ ■

*To the memory of
my Uncle and Godfather, Jerry Leff*

───────────────

**1927–1991**

# *Acknowledgments*

This book, like any other, is a group effort and I would like to thank everyone who contributed.

- Dianne King, acquisitions manager, for giving me the opportunity once again

- Joanne Cuthbertson, series editor, for her help in determining the overall structure and content of the book

- Brendan Fletcher, editor, who made a manuscript into a book and who was a pleasure to work with

- Joe Liburt, technical editor, who was an excellent critic and who made sure I got it right

- The word processors: Scott Campbell, Ann Dunn, Lisa Mitchell, Susan Trybull

- The members of Production, who built the book: Deborah Maizels, typesetter, Lisa Haden, proofreader, Suzanne Albertson, artist, and Cuong Le, who produced the screens

- My colleagues Sharon Crawford, Christian Crumlish, and Nick Dargahi, whose helpful advice cleared up a number of difficulties

- The Sales and Marketing Departments, who got the book onto the shelves

- My family, both immediate and extended, for their continued love and encouragement

- And Linda, for everything

If I have missed anyone, I assure you it was unintentional and I offer my apologies in advance.

# SYBEX Up & Running Books

■ ■ ■ ■ ■ ■ ■ ■ ■ ■

The Up & Running series of books from SYBEX has been developed for committed, eager PC users who would like to become familiar with a wide variety of programs and operations as quickly as possible. We assume that you are comfortable with your PC and that you know the basic functions of word processing, spreadsheets, and database management. With this background, Up & Running books will show you in 20 steps what particular products can do and how to use them.

*Who this book is for*

Up & Running books are designed to save you time and money. First, you can avoid purchase mistakes by previewing products before you buy them—exploring their features, strengths, and limitations. Second, once you decide to purchase a product, you can learn its basics quickly by following the 20 steps—even if you are a beginner.

*What this book provides*

The first step usually covers software installation in relation to hardware requirements. You'll learn whether the program can operate with your available hardware as well as various methods for starting the program. The second step often introduces the program's user interface. The remaining 18 steps demonstrate the program's basic functions, using examples and short descriptions.

*Contents & structure*

A clock shows the amount of time you can expect to spend at your computer for each step. Naturally, you'll need much less time if you only read through the step rather than complete it at your computer.

*Special symbols & notes*

You can also focus on particular points by scanning the short notes in the margins and locating the sections you are most interested in.

In addition, three symbols highlight particular sections of text:

The Action symbol highlights important steps that you will carry out.

The Tip symbol indicates a practical hint or special technique.

The Warning symbol alerts you to a potential problem and suggestions for avoiding it.

We have structured the Up & Running books so that the busy user spends little time studying documentation and is not burdened with unnecessary text. An Up & Running book cannot, of course, replace a lengthier book that contains advanced applications. However, you will get the information you need to put the program to practical use and to learn its basic functions in the shortest possible time.

**We welcome your comments**

SYBEX is very interested in your reactions to the Up & Running series. Your opinions and suggestions will help all of our readers, including yourself. Please send your comments to: SYBEX Editorial Department, 2021 Challenger Drive, Alameda, CA 94501.

# *Preface*

■ ■ ■ ■ ■ ■ ■ ■

Since its release in 1982, the Norton Utilities package has been the most popular utilities collection on the market. The reason for this is simple: No other software package so efficiently and comprehensively fills the gaps in DOS.

Now, the addition of several major programs in version 5.0 makes the Norton Utilities package more valuable than ever. If you have accidentally deleted a file with the DOS DEL command, you can use Norton's UNERASE to recover it. If you format a disk by mistake, thereby deleting its contents, you can use the UNFOR-MAT program to recover your data. In addition to these and other data recovery programs, the Norton Utilities include data security programs, hard disk optimization programs, and basic utility tools.

This book will get you "up and running" with the Norton Utilities as quickly as possible. In 20 short steps, you will become familiar with the most important and useful features of each of the programs.

To this end, most steps in this book contain a tutorial on a single program (in a few cases related programs have been grouped together). Begin by working through Step 1, which explains installation procedures, and Step 2, which shows you how to navigate the user interface. Once you've completed these steps, you'll be ready to read the remaining steps in any order that strikes your fancy. Step 3 covers the Norton Utilities Shell. Steps 4–8 treat data recovery programs, 9–11 discuss data security, 12–17 cover basic utility tools, and 18–20 show you how to improve your computer's speed.

When you have completed all 20 steps, you will have a solid grasp of the fundamentals of the Norton Utilities 5.0 and the ability to work more quickly, efficiently, and confidently with DOS.

Michael Gross

# Table of Contents

■ ■ ■ ■ ■ ■ ■ ■ ■ ■

**(30)** *Step 1*

Installation  1

**(15)** *Step 2*

The User
Interface  9

**(30)** *Step 3*

The Norton
Utilities Shell  17

**(45)** *Step 4*

Unerasing
Files  27

**(30)** *Step 5*

Formatting
and Unformatting  35

**(15)** *Step 6*

The Norton
Disk Doctor II  41

**(15)** *Step 7*

Repairing Damaged
Data Files  47

**(30)** *Step 8*

Miscellaneous
Recovery Tools  51

**(60)** *Step 9*

Data
Encryption  59

**(15)** *Step 10*

Monitoring
Disk Access  69

**(15)** *Step 11*

Destroying Data  75

**(30)** *Step 12*

Viewing and
Editing Data  81

**(30)** *Step 13*

Finding Files  89

**(15)** *Step 14*

Basic System
Configuration  97

**(30)** *Step 15*

Managing
Directories  105

**(15)** *Step 16*

Configuration
Information  111

**(45)** *Step 17*

Enhancing
Batch Files  119

**(60)** *Step 18*

Optimizing Your
Hard Disk I  133

**(45)** *Step 19*

Optimizing Your
Hard Disk II  141

**(15)** *Step 20*

Disk
Caching  149

# *Installation*

Before you can use the Norton Utilities for the first time, you must install them. While a few of the programs can be copied directly from the distribution disks, the majority of them, as well as all of the programs' supporting files, are archived and must be unpacked before use. Installation is most easily accomplished using the installation program that comes with the software. It is a straightforward procedure and should take you approximately 30 minutes, less if you choose not to install some optional features.

The Norton Utilities 5 comes on both 5¼- and 3½-inch disks. The installation procedure is nearly the same for both, differing only in the number of times you have to swap disks.

## HARDWARE REQUIREMENTS

In order to run the Norton Utilities, your system must be of the following minimal configuration:

■  An IBM PC, XT, AT, 386, PS/2 or 100%-compatible machine.

- DOS 2.0 or later.

- 512K of RAM.

- A hard disk is strongly recommended. Though it is, strictly speaking, possible to install the Norton Utilities on floppy disks, this step assumes you are installing to a hard disk.

## SELECTING OPTIONS

For the sake of economy and clarity, the installation instructions will tell you to select a particular option. This can mean selecting an option from a pull-down menu, selecting an item from a list, or selecting an option from a group of options on a dialog box.

*Mouse*
*versus*
*keyboard*

To select an option with the mouse, move the mouse pointer onto the option you want and click the left button. To select an option with the keyboard, highlight the option you want using the Tab key and arrow keys and press Enter. If more explicit instructions are needed in any particular step, they will be provided there. For a more complete discussion of selecting and the Norton Utilities interface in general, see Step 2.

## MAIN INSTALLATION

To install the Norton Utilities, follow these steps:

1. Place the disk marked Installation Disk in drive A.

2. Type

   `a:install`

   and press the Enter key.

*Display*
*options*

3. Select the *Black & White* option if you have a monochrome display or are using a laptop. Select the *Color* option if you have a color display.

4.  If you see a warning dialog box (users who are reinstalling the program may not), select the *Continue* option. (This dialog box warns you against installing the Norton Utilities if your hard disk has just been accidentally formatted or files you wish to recover have just been erased. Installing the Norton Utilities in such circumstances may prevent you from undoing them.)

5.  If you see an information dialog box (again, users who are reinstalling the program may not), select the *Continue* option. (This dialog box gives a brief overview of the installation process.)

6.  Select the *New Install* option if you are installing the Norton Utilities for the first time. Later, if you want to change any of the available configuration options, you can reinstall the program. If you are reinstalling the program for any reason, select the *Reconfigure* option and skip to the "Configuration Options" section below.

7.  Select the *Full Install* option if you want to install the entire Norton Utilities package. You should select *Full Install* unless your hard disk does not have the required space available or you are installing to floppies. If either of these two circumstances applies, select *Partial Install*.

    ■   If you select *Partial Install*, you will see a dialog box listing all of the programs that constitute the Norton Utilities. You can install any combination of these programs by selecting the ones you want. An *x* or check mark next to the program name indicates that the program is marked for installation. The amount of space that the marked programs will occupy when installed is prominently displayed. This total is updated each time you mark or unmark a program.

*Full installation versus partial installation*

*Installing
to the
NORTON
directory*

When you have marked (or unmarked) all of the programs you want, select the *Continue* option.

8.  Select the drive you are using to install the Norton Utilities. Drive A should already be highlighted. If it is not, use the ↑ or ↓ keys to highlight it and press Enter.

9.  The Norton Utilities will, by default, install to a directory named NORTON on drive C, unless it finds that you have a previous version of the software already installed. If you do not have a previous version installed, you can simply select the *Continue* option, wait while the program files are unarchived and copied, and then proceed to the next step. If, however, you do have a previous version installed, the installation program will suggest that the programs be installed in the directory containing the previous version. You then have several options:

    ■  If the suggested directory is acceptable, select the *Continue* option, at which point you will have the option of saving or overwriting the previous version. Select the *Back Up Files* option to do the former. Select the *overwrite Files* option to do the latter.

    ■  If the suggested directory is not acceptable, type the drive and path name you want instead. For example, to install the programs to a directory called NORTON on your drive D, you would type

    **D:\NORTON**

    When you have typed the drive and path name, select the *Continue* option. If you entered a directory other than the one suggested, you must select the *Continue* option again to confirm this. The files will then be unarchived and copied from the Installation Disk.

10. When the program is finished unarchiving and copying, it will prompt you for another disk. Place the disk you are

prompted for in the drive indicated and select the *Continue* option. Files will again be unarchived and copied.

11. Repeat step 10 until you are no longer prompted to insert disks.

12. When you are finished inserting disks, you will have the option of giving up to five programs shorter, mnemonic names. Select the programs you want to rename and then select the *Continue* option. Programs selected for renaming will be marked with an *x* or check mark. If you do not want to rename any programs, just select *Continue*. (If you do rename your programs, note that all programs will be called by their full, unabbreviated names throughout the book.)

*Renaming programs*

13. You now have the option of changing your default format program from DOS's FORMAT.COM to the Norton SFORMAT.EXE (Safe Format) program. (SFORMAT is the more capable format program, and it contains an important data protection feature. For a more complete discussion of this program, see Step 5.) If you want to use Safe Format, select the *Continue* option. The installation program will then rename the DOS program XXFORMAT.COM and the Norton program FORMAT.COM. If you don't want to use Safe Format, select the *Skip This* option.

*Safe Format*

Your screen should now look like Figure 1.1.

## CONFIGURATION OPTIONS

The Norton Utilities installation program provides the following configuration options:

- The *Password* option allows you to limit access to selected programs. See "Password Protection" below.

- The *Norton Program* option allows you to edit the program list in the Norton Utilities shell (the NORTON.EXE program). This program is discussed in Step 3 and the program list will be modified in the exercises there.

- The *Hardware* option allows you to set the video mode and mouse options. As this procedure is identical to the one found in the NORTON.EXE program, it will be discussed in Step 3 and not here.

- The *System Files* option lets you make changes to your AUTOEXEC.BAT and CONFIG.SYS files. For further discussion, see "Modifying Your Path" below.

## Password Protection

If you would like to password protect some of the Norton programs, select the *Password* option.

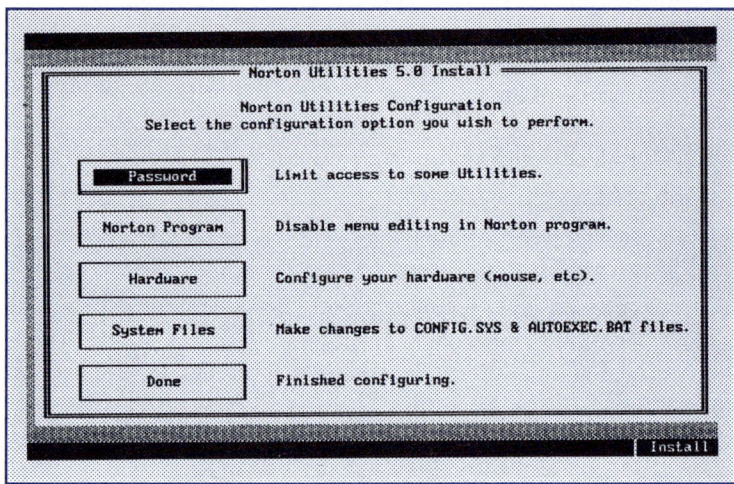

- *Figure 1.1: The Configuration Options screen*

1. In the dialog box that appears, select the programs that you wish to require password access. Selected programs are marked with an *x* or a check mark. When you are finished, select the *Continue* option.

2. Type a password and press Enter. The same password is used to protect all of the programs selected in the previous step.

3. Retype your password—to make sure you got it right—and press Enter. You are now back at the menu shown in Figure 1.1.

## Modifying Your Path

The last step you should take is to modify your path statement so that it includes the name of the subdirectory containing the Norton Utilities. (The remaining steps in this book assume that you have done so.) The path is simply a list of directories that DOS will check when you tell it to run a program. If the program you want to run is in one of the subdirectories on the list, it will execute. If it is not, you will get the familiar

```
bad command or filename
```

error. Putting the Norton Utilities' subdirectory on the path allows you to run the Norton programs from any DOS prompt.

To modify your path, do the following:

1. Select the *System Files* option from the Configuration Options screen.

2. Select the *AUTOEXEC.BAT* option. The command that sets your path is usually found in your AUTOEXEC.BAT file. Commands in AUTOEXEC.BAT are executed each time you boot the machine. This way, each time you start or restart the computer, your path is properly set.

3.  Select the *Continue* option on the information dialog box that appears.

4.  Select the *Add* option to automatically place the directory containing the Norton Utilities in your path.

5.  On the next screen, select the *Add* option again. This automatically creates what is called a DOS environment variable, which simply allows the Norton programs to find any necessary supporting files.

6.  Select the *Skip* option as you don't yet want to automatically load the DISKMON.EXE (Disk Monitor) or FILESAVE (File Save) programs. Loading these programs will be addressed in Steps 4 and 10.

7.  Select the *Skip* option again as you don't yet want to automatically load the Image program either. Loading this program will be addressed in Step 5.

8.  Again select the *Skip* option as you don't yet want to automatically run one of the tests from the NDD (Norton Disk Doctor II) program. This option will be addressed in Step 6.

9.  Select the *Save* option to record the change made to your AUTOEXEC.BAT file (i.e., your path statement). This returns you to the menu shown in Figure 1.1.

10. If you do not wish to install any of the other available program or configuration options, select *Done*. On the next screen, select the *Reboot* option.

Installation is now complete.

# *The User Interface*

This step details the Norton Utilities interface, the means by which you perform various program functions. The interface consists of dialog boxes, pull-down menus, full-screen and dialog box menus, toggle options and radio buttons, lists, and prompts for text. The interface can be navigated either with a mouse or with the keyboard, though in many instances a mouse is easier. As all but three of the programs in the package have the kind of interactive interface described in this step, you can refer back to these instructions as necessary.

## PULL-DOWN MENUS

Approximately half of the programs in the Norton Utilities have pull-down menus. The names of the available pull-down menus in a program are arranged horizontally across the top of the screen on the menu bar. A typical example from the NORTON.EXE program is shown in Figure 2.1.

*Selecting
with the
mouse*

To pull down a menu with the mouse, move the mouse pointer up to the menu bar and onto the name of the menu you want. Then click the left mouse button once. To select an option on this menu, move the mouse pointer onto the option you want and click the left mouse button once.

*Selecting
with the
keyboard*

To pull down a menu with the keyboard, hold down the Alt key and press the capitalized letter in the menu's name. For example, in Figure 2.1, Alt-C was pressed to pull down the Configure menu. To select an option on the menu, use the ↑ and ↓ keys to highlight the option you want and press Enter. Alternatively, you can simply press the capitalized, highlighted letter in the option you want. For example, in Figure 2.1, you would press **T** to select the *sort by Topic* option.

Many of the more common functions also have built-in shortcut key combinations. Pressing this key combination is equivalent to

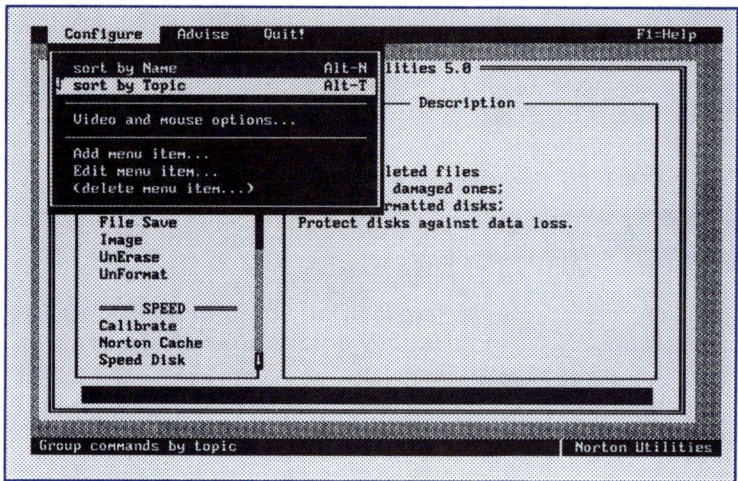

■ *Figure 2.1: A menu bar with one menu pulled down*

pulling down the menu and selecting the option. You can, therefore, accomplish in one step the same thing you normally accomplish in two. If a function has such a shortcut key combination, it
will appear next to the option on the pull-down menu.

## FULL-SCREEN AND DIALOG BOX MENUS

These two kinds of menu are essentially the same; they just appear
in different places. When a full-screen menu appears, it is usually
the first thing you see when you start a program. Full-screen
menus consist of a list of four to six rectangular options, usually
arranged horizontally or vertically, occupying the entire screen. A
dialog box menu shares the same possibilities of arrangement,
though it usually has fewer choices and appears inside a dialog
box along with other things: toggle options, text, etc. The *Save*
and *Cancel* options in Figure 2.2 constitute a dialog box menu.

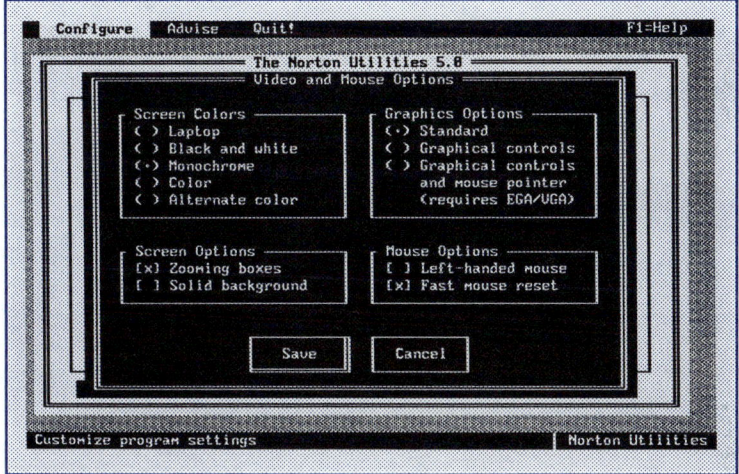

▪ *Figure 2.2: A dialog box with menu, toggle options, and radio buttons*

To select an option from a full-screen or dialog box menu, simply place the mouse pointer on the option you want and click the left mouse button once.

To select an option with the keyboard, use the arrow keys to highlight the option you want and press Enter. If you are in a dialog box, you may need to press the Tab key until one of the options in the menu is highlighted, as the cursor may be elsewhere within the dialog box (on toggle options, etc.).

The options on full-screen and dialog box menus, like the options on pull-down menus, also can be selected by pressing a "key" letter. Once any one of the options on the menu is highlighted, pressing the capitalized letter of the option you want is equivalent to highlighting it and pressing Enter.

## TOGGLE OPTIONS AND RADIO BUTTONS

These two kinds of options are quite similar and are used for program configuration. Toggle options are, as their name suggests, options that you can toggle between on and off only. Radio buttons are a *group* of options that, like the buttons on car radios before the advent of digital tuners, are mutually exclusive—selecting one automatically turns the others off. Both of these options often, but not always, appear on dialog boxes within named boxes, as in Figure 2.2. The options within the Screen Colors and Graphics Options boxes are radio buttons. The options within the Screen Options and Mouse Options boxes are toggles.

*Selecting with the mouse*

To select a toggle or radio button with the mouse, place the mouse pointer on the option's name and click the left button once. When on, a toggle will be marked with an *x* or a check mark and a radio button will be marked with a circle.

STEP 2

The procedure for selecting toggles and radio buttons with the keyboard differs slightly between the two kinds of options. To select a toggle, press the Tab key until the cursor appears at the option you want, then press **X** or the Spacebar to turn the option on or off. To select a radio button, press the Tab key until the cursor appears on one of the options in the group containing your option. Then press the Spacebar to cycle through the options until yours is selected.

*Selecting with the keyboard*

## LISTS

Sometimes you will need to select an item from a list. Often this will be a file, directory, or drive letter. Such lists appear in named boxes as in Figure 2.3.

*Selecting with the mouse*

To select an item from a list with the mouse, simply place the mouse pointer on the item you want and double-click the left

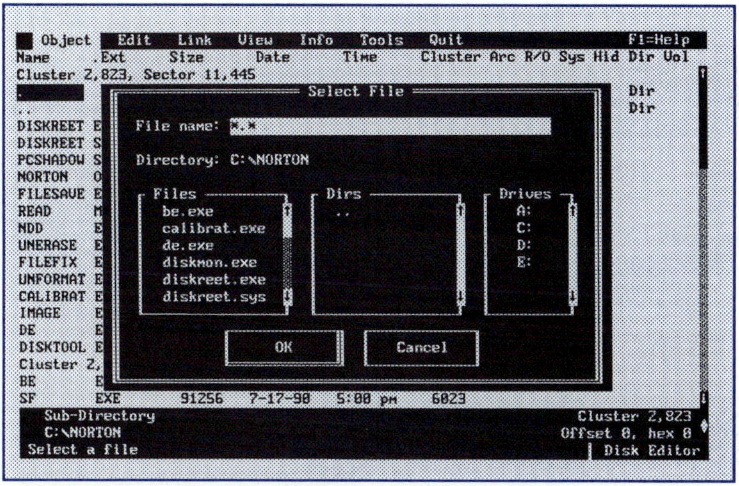


■ *Figure 2.3: A dialog box with lists*

mouse button. On many systems, clicking the right mouse button once has the same effect. If the list contains more items than can be displayed at once, you can scroll the list by means of the scroll bar on the right side of the list box. Placing the mouse button on one of the up or down arrows located at the top and bottom of the scroll bar scrolls the list in the direction indicated.

*Selecting*
*with the*
*keyboard*

To select an item from a list with the keyboard, highlight it using the ↑ and ↓ keys and press Enter. If the list contains more items than can be displayed at once, pressing the Home key moves you to the beginning of the list and pressing the End key moves you to the end. Pressing PageUp or PageDn scrolls the list a group of names at a time.

## PROMPTS

Occasionally within dialog boxes you will be asked to enter text at a prompt. Figure 2.3 displays a prompt called *File name:*. To enter text at a prompt, you must first move the cursor to the prompt, either by placing the mouse pointer at the prompt and clicking the left button or by repeatedly pressing the Tab key. Once the cursor is correctly positioned, simply type the desired text. In prompts, most of the standard editing keys are recognized: the Delete key deletes the character at the cursor, the Home and End keys move the cursor to the beginning and end of the typed text, and the ← and → keys move the cursor one character in the direction indicated.

## FINAL CONSIDERATIONS

There are a few, final, general points to keep in mind when working with the Norton Utilities interface.

■   Selecting Cancel or pressing the Esc key from any dialog box cancels it and its concomitant operation. If you ever need to change your mind, you always have the option of doing so.

- There are often multiple ways to perform the same operation (in addition to the simple mouse/keyboard dichotomy). Since the different methods are equivalent, use the one you are most comfortable with. For example, selecting the *OK* option on dialog box menus is equivalent to pressing Enter.

# *The Norton Utilities Shell*

The first program you might like to get acquainted with is NORTON, the Norton Utilities Shell. This program is a "central command center" for the Norton Utilities, which users of the Norton Utilities 4.5 will recognize as an expanded version of the Norton Integrator (NI) program. It lists all of the Norton programs, giving a description and syntax for each, and allows you to run them just as you would from the DOS prompt. However, when you run a program from the Shell, you return to the Shell when the program finishes executing. Working with NORTON, then, makes running the Norton Utilities somewhat easier. However, you can run them from the DOS prompt if you wish.

This step is a self-contained tutorial on the NORTON program and it covers not only running programs, but also sorting the list of programs, adding programs and topics to the list, and using NORTON to configure your display and your mouse. It should take you about 30 minutes to complete.

# STARTING NORTON

The first thing to do is, of course, to start the program.

If, during installation, you added the directory containing the Norton Utilities to your path, simply type

```
norton
```

and press Enter. If the directory containing the Norton Utilities is not on your path, then you must first change to the directory that does contain them. For example, if the programs reside in a directory called UTILS, first type

```
cd\utils
```

and press Enter to change to the UTILS directory. Then type

```
norton
```

and press Enter.

When the program starts, you will see the screen shown in Figure 3.1.

All of the Norton programs are listed in the Commands box on the left side of the screen. Use the ↑ and ↓ keys to scroll up and down the list. Note that the contents of the Description box change as the highlight bar moves from program name to program name.

# SORTING THE LIST OF PROGRAMS

When the NORTON program starts, the list of programs in the Commands box is sorted into four categories: RECOVERY, which groups programs used for data recovery; SPEED, which groups programs used to improve the overall performance of your system; SECURITY, which groups programs used to protect your data; and TOOLS, which is a collection of useful utility programs.

You may, however, prefer that the list be sorted alphabetically by file name. To sort alphabetically, pull down the Configure menu and select the *sort by Name* option, or just press Alt-N. The topic headings will disappear and the list will rearrange itself alphabetically.

Now change the list back so that it is sorted by topic once again. Pull down the Configure menu and select the *sort by Topic* option, or just press Alt-T. The topic headings reappear and the program names are rearranged alphabetically under each topic heading. The list of programs should remain sorted by topic for the rest of the exercise.

**Sorting by file name**

**Sorting by topic**

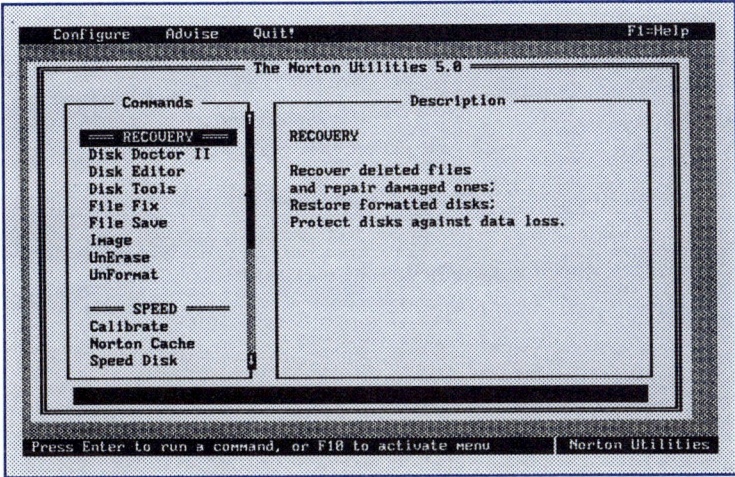

■ *Figure 3.1: The Norton Utilities Shell*

# RUNNING A PROGRAM

Having sorted and resorted the list of programs, you will find that running a program from the Shell is almost as simple. Minimally, all that is involved is highlighting the name of the program you want to run and pressing Enter or placing the mouse pointer on the name and double-clicking the left button. As an example, let's run the System Information program.

1. Move the highlight bar down to *System Info* and press Enter. *System Info* is at the bottom of the list of programs under the TOOLS topic. The System Information program will run and you will see the System Summary screen.

2. Now quit the program by selecting *Quit!* from the menu bar. You will return to the Shell with the highlight bar still on *System Info,* as in Figure 3.2.

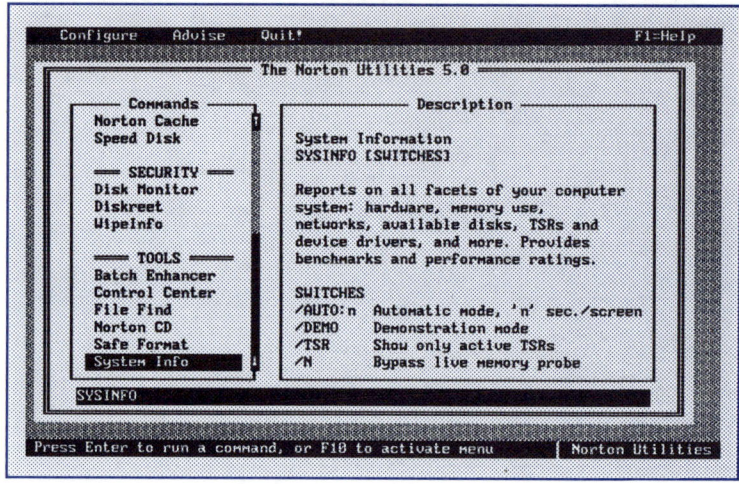

■ *Figure 3.2: The Shell with* System Info *highlighted*

## USING OPTIONAL PROGRAM SWITCHES

Notice that when you ran the System Information program above, you did not use any of the optional program switches that are listed for this program in the Description box. It is possible to run a program from the Shell using any of its switches, just as you could if you were running the program from the DOS command line.

Below the Commands box on your screen, you should see SYSINFO followed by a blinking cursor. (You will see SI if you shortened the SYSINFO filename to SI during installation.) To use optional switches when running a program from the Shell, simply type them here after you highlight the program's name on the list, but before you press Enter to execute the program. Since the program you want to run is already highlighted, go ahead and type

```
/auto:5
```

and then press Enter. The System Information program will run again, but this time it will automatically cycle through information screens at five second intervals, as specified by the /auto switch. After a few screens have gone by, press the Escape key to quit the program and return to the Shell.

## MODIFYING THE LIST OF PROGRAMS

Should you wish to put the Shell into frequent use, you will find that it is not limited to running only the Norton Programs. It is possible to add both topics and programs to the Shell, thereby making it usable as an everyday DOS shell. As an example, you will first add a new topic to the list called DOS, and then you will add the CHKDSK program beneath this topic.

## Adding a Topic to the List

In order to add a topic, the list must be sorted by topic and not by program name. If it is currently sorted by name, resort it by topic using the instructions in the section "Sorting the List of Programs."

1.   Pull down the Configure menu and select the *Add menu item...* option.

2.   On the dialog box that appears, select the *Topic* option.

3.   Another dialog box will appear with a list of current topics topped by a blank. Type

     **DOS**

     in the blank.

4.   You can use the ↑ and ↓ keys to position the new topic relative to the others. Press ↓ repeatedly until DOS is positioned below TOOLS.

5.   Press Enter or select the *OK* option to put your new topic into the list.

## Adding a Program to the List

Now that you have added the new topic, go ahead and add the new program.

1.   Using the ↑ and ↓ keys, highlight the topic under which you want the program to appear. (DOS should probably be highlighted as you just added it.)

2.   Pull down the Configure menu and select the *Add menu item...* option.

3.   On the dialog box that appears, select the *Command* option. This brings up another dialog box where you specify the

details of the program you are adding (its file name, the topic to which it belongs, etc.).

4. At the *name in menu:* prompt, where the cursor is positioned when the dialog box appears, type the program's name as you want it to appear on the program list:

   `Check Disk`

5. At the *DOS command:* prompt, type the program's file name:

   `CHKDSK`

6. In the Topics box containing a set of radio buttons, one for each available topic, press the Spacebar until the topic you want (DOS) is selected.

7. Press Enter or select the *OK* option to add the CHKDSK command to the list of programs under the DOS topic.

To make the NORTON program into an everyday DOS shell, you may want to take the time to add all of your frequently used DOS programs and applications to the program list. Then add the command

   `norton`

as the last line of your AUTOEXEC.BAT file. This will bring up your new DOS shell each time you start your computer.

## CONFIGURING YOUR DISPLAY AND MOUSE

You have now seen most of the major functions of the NORTON program, and the tutorial section of this step is essentially over. It may be useful to you, however, to know how to reset some options for your mouse and display if you find the default selections inadequate.

To reset these options, pull down the Configure menu and select the *Video and mouse options...* option. Then select according to Table 3.1. When you are finished configuring, select the *Save* option to make your changes permanent.

| Option | Description |
|--------|-------------|
| Laptop | Sets display for laptops |
| Black and White | Sets display for composite monitors |
| Monochrome | Sets display for monochrome monitors |
| Color | Sets display for color monitors |
| Alternate Color | Sets display on a color monitor for an alternate color set |
| Zooming Boxes | When enabled, causes boxes to "explode" or expand out from their centers when drawn |
| Solid background | Toggles between a solid on-screen background (ON) and a tiled background (OFF) |
| Standard | Marks and draws radio buttons and toggle options in text mode. Uses "block" mouse pointer |
| Graphical controls | Marks and draws radio buttons and toggle options in graphics mode. Uses "block" mouse pointer. Requires EGA/VGA |
| Graphical controls and mouse pointer | Marks and draws radio buttons and toggle options in graphics mode. Uses graphical "arrow" mouse pointer. Requires EGA/VGA |

*Table 3.1: Video and mouse options*

| Option | Description |
|--------|-------------|
| Left-handed mouse | Reverses mouse button functions for left-handed mouse users |
| Fast mouse reset | When enabled, turns on automatic, proper mouse pointer positioning |

*Table 3.1: Video and mouse options (continued)*

## QUITTING NORTON

When you are finished and want to quit the shell, select *Quit!* from the menu bar.

# *Unerasing Files*

Every computer user has, at one time or another, unintentionally deleted files or had it done for him or her. The ability to recover or "unerase" deleted files may be the most important, and is certainly the most desired, feature in all of the Norton Utilities.

Unerasing is possible because of the way DOS organizes your disks. When you delete a file, DOS considers the space the file occupied to be available again for use, and it will eventually write a new file or files onto that space. The data contained in the erased file is not destroyed, however; it remains on the disk. The erased file, then, can be recovered intact as long as no new files have been written over its data.

This step contains a tutorial on unerasing files with the Norton UNERASE program. You will create a short text file, delete it, and then unerase it. This step also contains a section on the FILE-SAVE program, which you can use to virtually guarantee successful unerasure of deleted files. It should take you about 45 minutes to work through this step.

## MAKING AND DELETING AN EXAMPLE FILE

Follow these steps to create and delete your example file:

1. Using your word processor of choice, type the following text at a blank or new screen:

   **This file will be used to test the Norton UNERASE program. It will be created, deleted, and unerased.**

2. Save the file using the file name C:\TEST.TXT. This will save the file to the root directory on your hard disk. (Save the file in ASCII or Text format if you know how, as this will make it easier to see the file's contents later. If you don't know how, don't worry about it.)

3. Once you have saved the file, quit your word processor.

4. Go to the root directory on you hard disk by entering

   **cd\**

5. Delete the file you have just created by entering the command

   **del test.txt**

## THE UNERASE PROGRAM

Start the UNERASE program by entering

**unerase**

at the DOS prompt or by selecting *UnErase* under the RECOVERY topic in the Norton Utilities Shell. Initially, you will probably see a list of subdirectories, but if you scroll down the list you will see a screen resembling the one in Figure 4.1. It displays the names of all of the erased files in the current directory as well as the names of any existing, nonerased subdirectories.

Notice that the first letter of each erased file name is missing. This is an artifact of DOS's bookkeeping. Erased files lose the first character in their names. This first character must be resupplied when the file is unerased.

Though the figure displays only one deleted file and no subdirectories, your screen may show many more. If your screen does not display the name of the erased sample file (?EST.TXT), and it very well may not, it is because the current directory is not the root directory. The current directory is identified at the top of the screen where it says *Erased files in....* If your current directory is not the root directory, that is, if the top of your screen does not

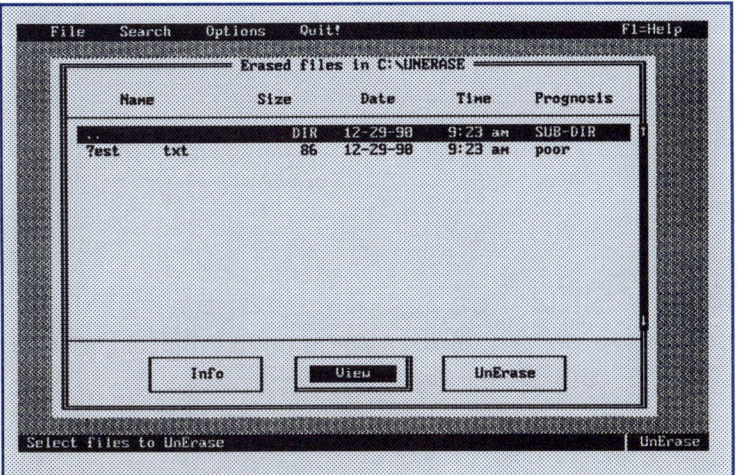

■ *Figure 4.1: A sample UNERASE screen*

say *Erased files in C:\,* change to the root directory as follows:

1.  Pull down the File menu and select the *change diRectory...* option or just press

    `Alt-R`

2.  On the directory tree that appears, highlight *C:\* and press Enter or highlight and select the *OK* option.

Now the deleted sample file, ?EST.TXT, should appear somewhere on the screen. If it still doesn't, try scrolling down the list.

Alternatively, you could change the display so that all erased files on the disk are displayed rather than just those in the current directory. To do this, pull down the File menu and select the *view All directories* option, or just press Alt-A. The display should change to something resembling Figure 4.2. Each erased file name has the name of its directory next to it. ?EST.TXT, and any other erased file in the root directory, will be identified by a *C:\* next to the file name.

Now, change the display back to the current directory. Pull down the File menu and select the *view Current directory* option, or just press Alt-C. The display should return to the screen resembling Figure 4.1.

## UNERASING FILES

The actual procedure for unerasing a file is quite simple. Basically, you just "point and shoot."

1.  Highlight the name of the file you want to unerase (?EST.TXT).

2.  Select the *View* option to see the contents of the file you are about to unerase. This step is optional, but do it now anyway. You should see the text you typed when you created

the sample file. If there is any odd "garbage" before or after the text, there are two possible explanations:

- You did not save TEST.TXT in ASCII format when you created it. The garbage is just your word processor's formatting codes; it's perfectly normal.

- There was some stray data next to TEST.TXT on your disk and you are seeing it now. Ignore it. It will not be recovered with the file.

3. Select the *OK* option when you are finished viewing.

4. Select the *Unerase* option to unerase the file.

5. Since the first letter of the file name was lost when you erased the file, press **T** to restore it. It actually does not matter what letter you type, but the file name, once unerased, will start with the letter you type.

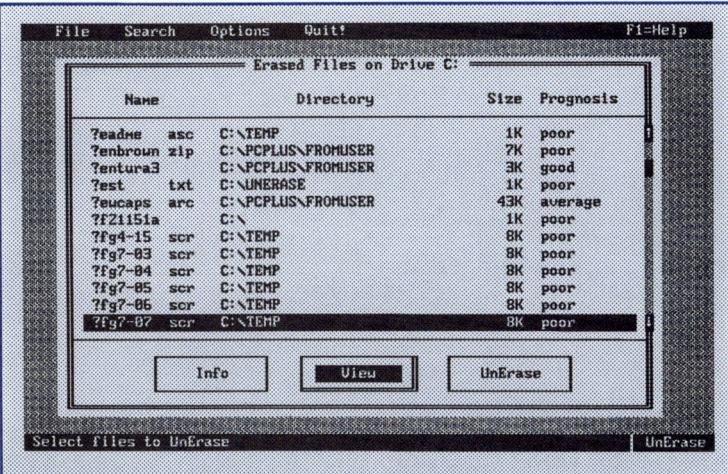

- *Figure 4.2: The UNERASE screen displaying all erased files on disk*

That's it! You have recovered the file. Notice that the first letter has been restored to the file name and that the file is listed as recovered under the Prognosis heading.

## QUITTING THE PROGRAM

You may unerase any number of files in a session by repeating the above procedure. Now that this exercise is finished, however, quit the program by selecting *Quit!* from the menu bar.

## THE FILESAVE PROGRAM

The FILESAVE program virtually guarantees successful unerasure by storing the data of deleted files in a special, hidden directory called TRASHCAN. "Erased" data is moved into this directory when a file is deleted so that it cannot be overwritten and destroyed when new files are put on the disk.

Using FILESAVE doesn't change the way you use UNERASE. That is, you will find erased files in the directories from which you deleted them, not in the TRASHCAN directory.

The remainder of this step will show you how to configure and use FILESAVE.

### Configuring FILESAVE

To configure the program, do the following:

1.  Start FILESAVE by entering

    `filesave`

    at the DOS prompt or by selecting *File Save* under the RECOVERY topic in the Norton Utilities Shell.

STEP

4

2. On the main program menu that appears, select the *Choose drives* option. This produces a dialog box listing all drives installed on your system.

3. Select any combination of drives you want to protect. Only files on the drives you select here will be moved into TRASHCAN when erased.

4. Select the *OFF* option.

5. Select the *File Protection* option from the main program menu.

6. On the dialog box that appears, toggle on the *Include archived (backed up) files* option. This protects files you have backed up with the DOS BACKUP command.

7. If you think five days is too short (or long) a time to hold deleted data before purging it, you can change this at the *Purge files held over* option.

8. Select the *OK* option to return to the main program menu.

9. Select *Quit* to quit the program and return to the DOS prompt.

These settings will be in effect each time you use the program and will remain in effect until you change them again.

## Using FILESAVE

FILESAVE is a memory-resident program that must be loaded into memory and activated in order to work. If you are only going to use it occasionally, enter

```
filesave /on
```

at any DOS prompt, or type **/on** before launching FILESAVE from the shell. It will remain in effect until you turn off (or re-boot) your computer or you issue a

`filesave /off`

command.

It makes more sense, however, to use FILESAVE all the time, if you are going to use it at all. The easiest way to do this is to load the program from your AUTOEXEC.BAT file. It will then be loaded and activated each time you start or restart your machine.

To load FILESAVE into memory, place the command

`filesave /on`

near or at the end of your AUTOEXEC.BAT file. You can use any word processor to do this.

Remember, though, that you *must* save your modified AUTOEXEC.BAT file in ASCII or Plain Text format. If you don't save your AUTOEXEC in ASCII format, DOS will not be able to read it correctly when you boot your machine.

# Formatting and Unformatting

■ ■ ■ ■ ■ ■ ■ ■ ■ ■ ■

New floppy disks must be formatted before they can be used, a procedure roughly analogous to grading a road before it can be paved. New hard disks must be formatted as well, though unlike floppies, most hard disks are formatted by the manufacturer or dealer before they arrive at your desk.

The formatting program provided with DOS, FORMAT, works perhaps a little too well. Formatting a disk with FORMAT has the side effect of irrevocably destroying any data on that disk. While this isn't a problem for brand new disks, as there is no data on them anyway, the accidental formatting of your current disks, particularly your hard disk, would result in catastrophic data loss.

Three of the Norton Utilities, SFORMAT (Safe Format), UNFOR-MAT, and IMAGE, are designed specifically for this situation. Disks formatted with the SFORMAT program or protected by the IMAGE program can be unformatted with UNFORMAT without loss of data. You should, therefore, seriously consider using SFORMAT in place of the DOS FORMAT program.

This step contains a tutorial on SFORMAT and UNFORMAT and provides instructions on the use of IMAGE. In the tutorial you will place sample files on a blank disk, reformat it, and then unformat it and recover the files. You should be able to work through this step in about 30 minutes.

## SFORMAT AND UNFORMAT

To start the tutorial you should have a blank, formatted disk in your A drive. If you need to format a new disk, go ahead and use the DOS FORMAT program this one last time.

### Creating a Sample Disk

Using your word processor of choice, create two sample files containing only a sentence or two of text. Save the first file under the name

`a:testfile.1`

and the second file under the name

`a:testfile.2`

These are the files that, over the remainder of the tutorial, will be lost with formatting and then recovered.

### Reformatting the Disk (Safely)

1.  Start the SFORMAT program by entering

    `sformat`

    or

    `sf`

at the DOS prompt (type the latter only if you renamed the program during installation). You can also launch the program from the Norton Utilities Shell by selecting the *Safe Format* option under the TOOLS topic. When the program starts, your screen should look like Figure 5.1.

2. In the box named Drive, highlight the drive to format (*A:*). If you are using the keyboard, use the ↑ and ↓ keys to highlight *A:,* but do not yet press Enter as this will start formatting the disk.

3. In the box called Size, select the capacity to which the disk will be formatted. Notice that you have a number of sizes from which to select. This allows you, for example, to format a double-density (360K 5¼-inch or 720K 3½-inch) disk in a high-density (1.2Mb 5¼-inch or 1.44Mb 3½-inch) drive. However, for the purposes of this exercise, let's keep things simple: select *360K* if your sample disk is 360K, and

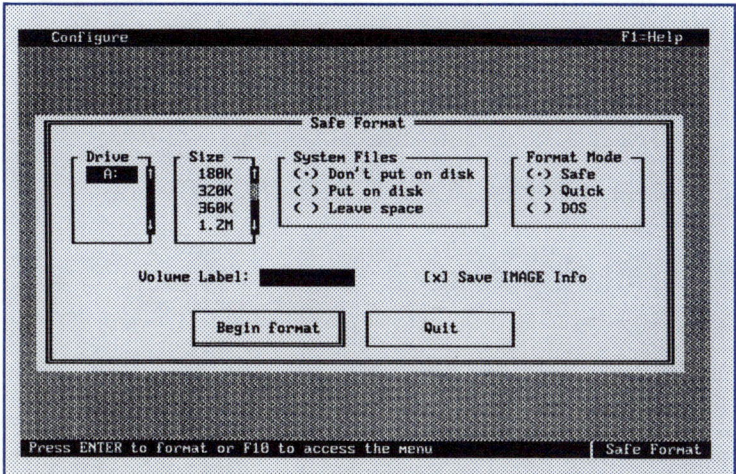

■ *Figure 5.1: The SFORMAT (Safe Format) program*

so on. Again, if you are using the keyboard, use the arrow keys to highlight your selection, but do not yet press Enter.

4. From the radio buttons in the System Files box, select the *Don't put on disk* option. You should always use this option unless you want to create a bootable disk, in which case you would select the *Put on disk* option.

5. From the radio buttons in the Format Mode box, select *Safe*. You should not select the *DOS* option here as this causes SFORMAT to work like the DOS FORMAT program.

6. Toggle the *Save IMAGE Info* option to on. This option is very important. If not toggled on, UNFORMAT may not be able to recover all of your data.

7. Now start disk formatting by selecting the *Begin Format* command from the menu at the bottom of the dialog box.

8. You will see a dialog box warning you that there is data on the disk that will be destroyed. The two files you created above should be listed. Select *Yes* to go ahead with the format.

9. You will be prompted when the disk is finished formatting. Select *OK* to acknowledge completion.

10. Quit SFORMAT by selecting the *Quit* option.

## Unformatting a Disk

Now check the contents of the sample disk in drive A by entering

```
dir a:
```

at the DOS prompt. The message *File not found* means the disk is blank. The two files you created and put on this disk have been overwritten by reformatting the disk. However, since the disk was formatted with SFORMAT and not the DOS FORMAT program, it is possible to unformat the disk and retrieve the files.

If one of your disks should ever be accidentally formatted, unformat it *immediately*. Do not put any new files on the disk. If you do, you will lose these new files when you unformat.

To unformat the disk in drive A, do the following:

1. Start the UNFORMAT program by entering

   `unformat`

   at the DOS prompt or by selecting the *UnFormat* option under the RECOVERY topic on the Norton Utilities Shell.

2. When the program starts, you will see an information dialog box. Select *Continue* when you are finished reading.

3. On the list that appears in the next dialog box, select the drive to unformat (*A:*) and then click on *OK* or press Enter.

4. In the response to the question on the next dialog box, *Did you use IMAGE.EXE...*, select *Yes*. Although strictly speaking, you did not run the IMAGE program on this disk, it is very important not to select *No*. Toggling on the *Save IMAGE info* in step 6 of the previous exercise performed the same function. (Both IMAGE and the *Save IMAGE info* option save critical disk information that allows a disk to be unformatted without data loss. See the discussion of IMAGE in the section below.)

5. Select *Yes* when asked if you are sure you wish to proceed.

6. Select *OK* to restore the formatted disk.

7. In the next dialog box, select *Yes* when prompted. This warning appears because unformatting a disk and restoring its original data will destroy any files written to the disk *after it was reformatted*.

8. Select *Full*. The disk will then be unformatted.

9. When UNFORMAT is finished, select *OK* to acknowledge completion.

10. Select the *Quit* option to leave the program and inspect your work.

If you look at the directory of drive A, you will see that the two sample files have been restored. If you wish, you can start your word processor again and retrieve the files to inspect their contents.

## IMAGE

As mentioned above, the IMAGE program, like SFORMAT's *Save IMAGE Info* option, allows UNFORMAT to restore data to a disk that was formatted. It does so by saving critical disk information—DOS's record of the contents of a disk—to a file called IMAGE.DAT. UNFORMAT then reads this file during its operation.

IMAGE is best used on your hard disk, though it works just as well on floppies. To run the program, simply enter **image** at the DOS command line, followed by the drive designator of the disk you want to protect, as in

```
image c:
```

In fact, you may want to place this command in your AUTOEXEC.BAT so that it will run every time you start or restart your computer. This way, you will always be protected from an accidental hard disk format on your machine.

# *The Norton Disk Doctor II*

The Norton Disk Doctor II (so called because there was a previous version of the program included with the Norton Utilities version 4.5) is a valuable and useful program; it checks your disks for errors and automatically fixes any that it finds.

In this step, you will use the Norton Disk Doctor II to check your hard disk for errors. Since the program is largely automated, this step should only take you about 15 minutes.

## RUNNING THE DISK DOCTOR

1.  Start the program by entering

    **ndd**

    at the DOS prompt. You can also launch the Disk Doctor from the Norton Utilities Shell by selecting the *Disk Doctor II* option under the RECOVERY topic.

2. From the program's main menu, select the *Diagnose Disk* option.

3. On the list that appears, select the drive you want to check (*C:*), and choose the *Diagnose* option. Note that it is possible to select multiple drives here. To do so, merely click the left mouse button on the drives you want or highlight the drive and press the Spacebar. A check mark indicates drives selected for diagnosis. If you have multiple hard disks, choose only drive C for this exercise.

4. The Doctor will begin diagnosing your disk, checking such items as the File Allocation Tables and directory structure—in short, all of the vital, logical organs of your hard disk. It is most unlikely that the Doctor will find any errors. If, however, some do turn up, you should instruct the Doctor to fix them. As explanations on errors and repairs are provided by the program, and as the Doctor makes all fixes automatically, all that is left to the user is to select *Continue* in response to any explanation and to select *Yes* in response to any prompt to correct an error.

5. When the diagnosis of essential, logical disk information is complete, whether or not any errors have been found, the screen should look like Figure 6.1.

If the Doctor is unable to fix an error, you may have a serious problem with your hard disk or some other, related part of your computer. You should contact your technical support department, dealer, or manufacturer.

**Running a surface test**

You can now run a surface test, which checks the surface of your disk for physical errors. These crop up somewhat more often than the logical errors discussed above and are comparatively minor. If the Doctor finds such errors, it will mark the affected area so that it can no longer be used and thus present no danger to your

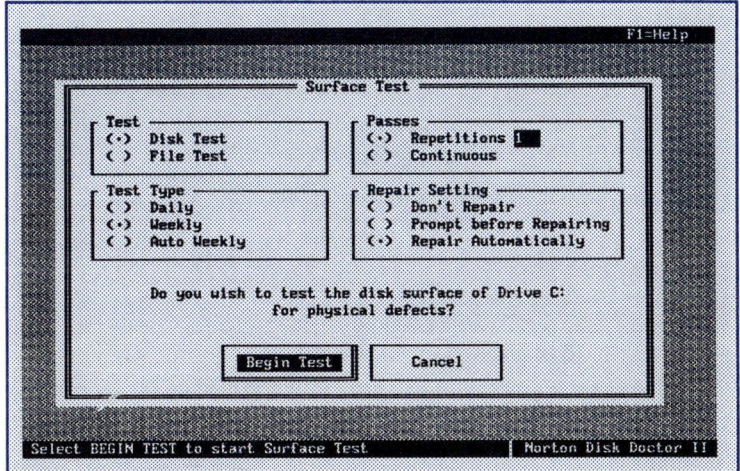

• *Figure 6.1: The Surface Test screen*

data. If data is currently sitting on the affected area, it will be moved to a healthy section of the disk.

Before running the surface test, make sure you select the appropriate options. These options are all radio buttons and should be set according to Table 6.1.

| Box | Option to select | Purpose |
|---|---|---|
| Test | Disk Test | Tests entire disk surface rather than only the space occupied by files |
| Passes | Repetitions 1 | Runs the surface test once (or the number of times specified here) rather than continuously until interrupted |

*Table 6.1: Surface test options*

| Box | Option to select | Purpose |
|---|---|---|
| Test Type | Weekly | Provides a sufficiently rigorous test to catch incipient physical errors |
| Repair Setting | Repair Automatically | Automatically fixes any physical errors found |

*Table 6.1: Surface test options (continued)*

Begin the surface test by selecting the *Begin Test* option at the bottom of the screen. When the surface test is finished (and any errors corrected) the Doctor displays a summary of its findings. If no errors were found, select the *Done* option.

***Disk Doctor reports***

If, however, errors were discovered, the summary information is available as a report. If the Doctor was unable to fix all errors found, this report will be useful to anyone you contact for technical support. To print a report, select the *Report* option followed by the *Print* option. Select the *Done* option when the report is finished printing.

Having returned to the main program menu, select the *Quit* option to quit the program.

## MAINTAINING YOUR DISKS

The Norton Disk Doctor II can check floppy disks as well as hard disks. You should run it under the following circumstances:

■ If a program reports that it is unable to read a file, DOS usually reports this as

```
Data error reading drive...
```

Be careful here. Being unable to *read* a file is different than being unable to *find* a file. The former usually means that there is some kind of physical error involved. The latter simply means that the program in which you are working can't find the file you want because it is somewhere else. This is not a serious error and does not require running the Disk Doctor.

■ Once every few months on your older floppy disks as preventative maintenance.

■ Once every few months on your hard disk as preventative maintenance. The Installation program gives you the option of running a partial diagnosis with the Disk Doctor every time you boot your machine. This really isn't necessary.

# *Repairing Damaged Data Files*

■ ■ ■ ■ ■ ■ ■ ■ ■ ■ ■

It occasionally happens that some of your data files are damaged, causing no small amount of anxiety and extra work. The FILEFIX program is capable of repairing, or at least rescuing, data from damaged files created by the more common applications. Specifically, it can repair Lotus 1-2-3 files (versions 1, 1A, and 2), dBASE files (versions II, III+, and IV), and Lotus Symphony files, as well as any files that are 100%-compatible with these (Clipper, Twin, etc.).

*File formats supported*

This step contains a short tutorial on how to automatically repair data files (FILEFIX contains some more advanced, manual repair functions for dBASE files, but these are beyond the scope of this step). There is no need to create damaged files, though if you happen to have some, so much the better. You should, however, have a healthy 1-2-3 spreadsheet (or Symphony file, as the repair procedures for 1-2-3 and Symphony are identical) and a healthy dBASE file for these exercises. The tutorial should only take you 15 minutes or so.

# REPAIRING 1-2-3 (OR SYMPHONY) FILES

You will begin the exercise by repairing a 1-2-3 (or Symphony) file. Do not worry about using healthy files, since FILEFIX creates a copy of the file it is working on. It does not overwrite the file itself. However, if using healthy files makes you uncomfortable, make a copy of your data files before you begin.

To repair the file, do the following:

1. Start the FILEFIX program by entering

   `filefix`

   at the command line or by selecting the *File Fix* option under the RECOVERY topic in the Norton Utilities shell.

2. When the program starts up, select the option representing the kind of file you are repairing (*1-2-3* or *Symphony*).

3. In the next dialog box that appears, you must provide the name of the file to repair. You can do this by typing the complete file name and path at the *File name:* prompt, as in

   `c:\123\costs.wk1`

   or you may select the file name from the Drives, Dirs, and Files lists. To do the latter, simply select, in order, the drive on which the file resides from the Drives box, the directory in which the file resides from the Dirs box, and then the file name itself from the Files box. Once you have selected the file name from the Files box, the name you have chosen appears at the file name prompt as if you had typed it. (If you do not see the directory you want listed in the Dirs box, select the .. directory. If your directory is still not listed, select .. until you find it. Most of the time you will not have to do this more than twice.)

4. Select the *OK* option on the dialog box menu.

5.  Now, at the *Repair...* prompt, you must provide the name
    that the fixed file will have. For this exercise, accept the
    default name FIXED and do nothing here. (If you will be
    fixing multiple files, do not use FIXED for each repair or
    else one file will overwrite another. Use a different file
    name for each. Moreover, if you do not accept the de-
    fault name, do not give the repaired file the same name as
    the damaged file. If you do, you will overwrite the
    damaged file.)

6.  On the same screen in the Repair Mode box, select the
    radio button called *Attempt recovery of all data* if it is not
    already selected. This allows you to reconstruct the entire
    spreadsheet. (If, however, you find that this does not work
    and you need to attempt the repair again, select the *Recover
    cell data only* radio button the next time through. This
    recovers the contents of cells but nothing else. This way,
    at least you'll have your data, although it will be
    unformatted.)

7.  Select the *Begin* option at the bottom of the dialog box to
    start repairs. When repairs are done, you should have a file
    named FIXED.

8.  FILEFIX can create a report detailing every cell repaired
    and recovered. As the report can be quite long, select the
    *No Report* option for the purposes of this exercise. How-
    ever, you could select the *Printer* option to print this report
    or the *File* option if you want the report sent to a disk file.

9.  Regardless of what option you selected in step 8, you will
    have the opportunity to repair another file. So that you will
    be able to do the next part of this exercise, select *Yes* when
    asked *Do you want to repair more files?*. This takes you
    back to the startup screen you saw after step 1. Selecting
    *No* here quits FILEFIX.

# REPAIRING DBASE FILES

When you have finished repairing your 1-2-3 or Symphony file, you should have been returned to the FILEFIX startup screen. To automatically repair your "damaged" dBASE file, follow these steps (which are similar to those detailed above):

1. Choose the *dBASE* option from the FILEFIX main screen.

2. Provide the name of the file to repair, as in step 3 above, and select *OK*.

3. In the next dialog box, again accept the default name FIXED for the repaired file and do nothing at the *Repair...* prompt.

4. On the same screen, select the radio button labeled *Fully automatic* in the Repair mode box.

5. Below the Repair Mode box, there are three toggle options. The default settings are acceptable. (The first option, *Use Clipper field limits,* should be off. Toggle it on only if you are repairing a Clipper database. The second and third options, *Fix shifted data automatically* and *Strict character checking,* should be toggled on.)

6. Select the *Begin* option at the bottom of the dialog box.

7. Select the *Skip Review* option to start repairs.

8. When repairs are finished, you will again have the option of printing a detailed report of FILEFIX's work. Again, select the *No Report* option.

9. To end the exercise and quit FILEFIX, select the *No* option when asked if you want to repair more files.

# Miscellaneous Recovery Tools

The DISKTOOL program is a collection of recovery functions that can fix problems ranging from the fairly common to the catastrophic. With DISKTOOL, you can

- Make bootable disks out of nonbootable disks

- Undo the mess created by running the DOS RECOVER program

- Reformat a floppy containing bad sectors without losing data

- Mark specific clusters as bad or good

- Save a copy of your critical system information just in case of disaster and then restore it if necessary

This step will take you through three of these five functions and treat the remaining two, which aren't commonly useful, in a brief, general discussion.

# MAKING A DISK BOOTABLE

You may sometimes find yourself wishing that a particular floppy disk were bootable. For example, the new peripheral you have just added to your system is not working. You need to boot your system from a floppy so that your usual complement of device drivers, which might be conflicting with your new peripheral, are not loaded when you start the machine.

**The DOS SYS program**

The DOS SYS program will make a floppy disk bootable, but, as you may have noticed if you have ever tried to use the SYS command, it really isn't that useful since the disk must be completely empty for the program to work. The problem is that the DOS system files—the hidden files that, when present, cause a disk to be bootable—must sit at the very beginning of a disk. The first file put on a nonbootable disk, however, is also placed at the beginning. When the SYS program tries to place the system files on a nonempty, nonbootable disk, it finds a file in the way and reports, misleadingly, that there is insufficient room for the system files. The *Make a disk bootable* function in DISKTOOL, however, is more sophisticated. It can relocate files from the beginning of a disk and then place the system files properly.

Let's begin the tutorial and make a bootable disk.

1.  Start DISKTOOL by entering

    `disktool`

    at the command line or by selecting the *Disk Tools* option under the RECOVERY topic in the Norton Utilities Shell.

2.  In the program summary dialog box that appears, select the *Continue* option when you are finished reading. This brings you to the DISKTOOL main screen, shown in Figure 8.1.

3.  From the Procedures list, highlight *Make a disk bootable*. Then select the *Proceed* option.

4.  From the list of drives that appears, select the drive containing the floppy you want to make bootable (*A:*) and select *OK*.

5.  Place a blank, nonbootable floppy disk in drive A (though in practice the disk does not have to be blank) and then select *OK*. This starts DISKTOOL. The process shouldn't take long.

6.  When DISKTOOL is finished, select *OK* to acknowledge completion and return to the main screen.

That's all there is to it, but don't quit the program to test the results just yet. Leave the disk in drive A and let's go on to the next function.

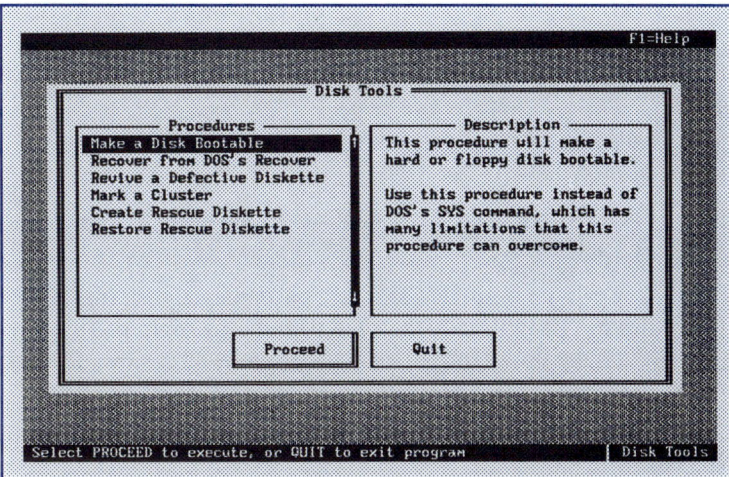

- *Figure 8.1: The DISKTOOL main screen*

# REVIVING A DEFECTIVE DISK

When one of the files on your disk cannot be read, you will likely see the cryptic DOS error message

`Sector not found error reading drive...`

The problem is that some of the disk's formatting information has, for one reason or another, been lost. When DOS formats a disk, it marks the disk up into discreet units—clusters and sectors. If this information is disturbed, DOS may not be able to find the files it is looking for. DISKTOOL fixes this problem by laying down new format information without destroying disk data.

If you see this bad sector error, you should try to fix the problem with the Norton Disk Doctor first. However, if this does not help, you can try to fix the disk with DISKTOOL. Note that this is *not* the same operation you saw in Step 5 with the Safe Format and IMAGE programs.

Assuming, then, that the disk still in drive A has bad sectors on it and that the Norton Disk Doctor did not work:

1.  Select the *Revive a defective diskette* option from the Procedures list.

2.  On the drive list that appears, select the drive to revive (*A:*) and select *OK*.

3.  You will be prompted to insert the damaged disk into drive A (it is already there). Select the *OK* option. This starts the program. The operation can be a bit slow, depending on the extent of the damage and the size of the disk.

4.  Select *OK* to verify completion and return to the main screen.

If the disk had truly been damaged, DISKTOOL would have allowed you to recover at least part of the corrupted data. Leave the disk in drive A once again for the last part of the tutorial.

# RESCUE DISKETTES

DISKTOOL gives you the ability to save some essential system information—your hard disk's partition table, the boot record, and CMOS data—to a floppy disk in case of disaster. It is most unlikely that any of this information will be lost. If this should happen, however, the information can then be copied back to your machine.

## Creating a Rescue Diskette

To make the disk in drive A into a rescue diskette:

1.  Select the *Create Rescue Diskette* option from the Procedures list.

2.  Select the *OK* option when you are finished reading the information box that appears.

3.  From the drive list, select the disk onto which the rescue files should be copied (*A:*) and select *OK*.

4.  When DISKTOOL is finished working, select the *OK* option to acknowledge completion and return to the main screen.

You now have a rescue disk, just in case. Take the disk from the drive and label it accordingly. The steps for restoring a rescue disk will be described in the next section, but it is not necessary to follow along at your machine.

## Restoring Rescue Information

You should always run the Norton Disk Doctor before restoring your rescue diskette. Resorting to DISKTOOL should really be your last option. If, however, the Norton Disk Doctor is ever unable to repair a damaged partition table or Boot Record, or if your CMOS information is ever lost, use DISKTOOL to copy this information back onto your machine.

1.  Select the *Restore Rescue Diskette* option from the Procedures list.

2.  Select the *Yes* option from the warning dialog box if you're absolutely certain you want to restore rescue information.

3.  In the dialog box that appears, you can select which part of the rescue information to restore by means of three toggle options. Toggle on the *partition Table* and *Boot Record* options if the Norton Disk Doctor has not been able to fix errors in these areas. Select *CMOS Values* if your machine has lost its configuration information. (Configuration information includes the kind of drives you have installed, the kind of video card you have, the amount of memory installed, etc. The most common symptom of lost CMOS information is the sudden inability of your machine to find its hard disk.) You can restore CMOS information in place of running your computer's Setup program. When you have toggled on the options you want, select the *OK* option.

4.  Put the rescue disk in drive A.

5.  From the drive list, select the drive from which to restore rescue information (*A:*) and select *OK*.

6.  Select the *Yes* option once for each kind of data toggled in step 3 above.

7.  When the rescue information has been copied back to your computer, remove the rescue disk from drive A and select the *Reset* option to reboot your machine. You must select the *Reset* option here for the information to have the desired effect.

If you believe there is a serious problem with your machine—if you have run the Disk Doctor first, then restored rescue information, and your machine still does not function properly—consider contacting technical support or your dealer.

## THE REMAINING DISKTOOL FUNCTIONS

There are two other functions in DISKTOOL. The *RECOVER from DOS's Recover* function undoes the damage done by the DOS program RECOVER. DOS's RECOVER is provided to salvage data from disks with corrupted directory structures, but it "works" poorly. If you've used DOS's RECOVER, use *RECOVER from DOS's RECOVER* to undo the mess of indistinguishable files RECOVER produces. If you have a disk with a damaged directory, use the Norton Disk Doctor instead.

The last function is *Mark as Cluster.* It allows you to mark a cluster as bad, thereby preventing any data from being written there, or as good, which returns a cluster marked bad to active duty. You should never have to use this option, really. The DOS FORMAT program and the Disk Doctor will mark damaged clusters as bad and remove them from use. If a cluster has been marked as bad and you mark it as good, you are jeopardizing your data, as it can then be written to this damaged space.

If you haven't done so already, quit DISKTOOL by selecting the *Quit* option on the main screen.

# *Data Encryption*

There are a number of situations where you may wish to keep your data private. In this and the following two steps, we will discuss several programs designed to keep your data away from prying eyes and safe from accidental deletion.

This step will cover the DISKREET program, which allows you to secure your data in two different ways. You can encrypt individual files, thereby rendering them unintelligible and useless to anyone without the password needed to unscramble them, or you can use DISKREET to create an encrypted *drive,* called an NDisk. A password is required to access an NDisk, thereby keeping safe any files stored there.

This step's tutorial is divided into two parts. In the first part, you will encrypt and decrypt a file. In the second part, you will create an NDisk. This tutorial is a bit more involved than those in any of the previous steps; it should take you about one hour.

# PREPARING FOR ENCRYPTION

In order for DISKREET's NDisk functions to be available to you when you run the program, the driver DISKREET.SYS must be loaded in your CONFIG.SYS file. This was one of the options you skipped over during installation. Therefore, before the tutorial actually begins, you must modify your system configuration.

Use your word processor to add the line

```
device=c:\norton\diskreet.sys
```

to your CONFIG.SYS file. When you have done this, save the file in ASCII format, as DOS will be unable to read it if you don't. Then reboot your computer.

As your machine is booting, it will beep, stop executing, and display a screen similar to that in Figure 9.1. This is just to alert you that DISKREET has no default settings and that a configuration file has been created. Simply press a key to continue. Subsequent system restarts will not be interrupted in this way.

When your system has finished booting, restart your word processor and create a small file that contains the following text:

```
This is the sample file used in Step 9 to test
DISKREET's data encryption.
```

```
DISKREET(tm)  1990 Peter Norton Computering, Inc.
All rights reserved.
No DISKREET config file to read (DISKREET.INI).
DISKREET's Main Password has been cleared.
Instant close keys have been reset to LEFT + RIGHT shift keys.
AUTO-CLOSE TIME-OUT interval has been set to five minutes and DISABLED.
Keyboard lock & screen blank has been DISABLED.
NDISK drive count set to one.

***************      PRESS  ANY  KEY  TO  CONTINUE      ***************
```

■ *Figure 9.1: DISKREET's automatic configuration*

Save the file under the name

`c:\norton\testfile`

# FILE ENCRYPTION AND DECRYPTION

With the necessary preliminaries out of the way, you are ready to begin encrypting and decrypting files. The first thing you will do is start the program and make one change in its configuration.

1.  Start the DISKREET program by entering

    **diskreet**

    at the command line or by selecting the *Diskreet* option under the SECURITY topic in the Norton Utilities Shell.

2.  On the dialog box that appears, select the *Files* option. This will pull down the File menu.

3.  Select the *File options...* option.

4.  Toggle the *Wipe/Delete original files after encryption* option on.

5.  Select the *Save* option at the bottom of the dialog box.

6.  Select *OK* to acknowledge the saving of new configuration information.

The above sequence makes (and saves) a necessary change in the way DISKREET works when encrypting. By default, DISKREET will encrypt a *copy* of the file you specify, leaving the original intact and defeating the program's own purpose. The option you just turned on tells DISKREET to destroy the original file after it is encrypted.

7.  The File menu should still be down. Select the *Encrypt...* option.

8. At the *File name:* prompt on the dialog box that appears, type the name, including path, of the file to encrypt

   `c:\norton\testfile`

   and press Enter.

9. You are now prompted to enter the name the file should have *after* it is encrypted. DISKREET suggests

   `c:\norton\testfile.sec`

   Press Enter or select *OK* to accept this.

10. You now must enter the password required to decrypt the file when you wish to use it. Type

    `stepnine`

     and press Enter. *Do not forget the password you assign to an encrypted file. You cannot access the file without this password!*

11. Now reenter the password. This is necessary to make sure that the encrypted file is assigned the password you intended. When you have done this, the program goes to work.

12. Select *OK* to acknowledge completion of the encryption.

Now quit DISKREET by selecting the *Quit!* option on the menu bar. Examine the file by typing **testfile.sec** at the command line or trying to call it into your word processor. The result should look something like Figure 9.2.

You can see how powerful file encryption is. The contents of this file are quite safe—useless in its current state, but quite safe.

Now let's decrypt TESTFILE.SEC and return the file to use.

*Decryption*

1.  Restart DISKREET.

2.  Select the *Files* option on the first dialog box.

3.  This time select the *Decrypt...* option from the File menu.

4.  At the *File name:* prompt on the dialog box that appears, type the name, including path, of the file to decrypt

    `c:\norton\testfile.sec`

    and press Enter.

5.  Enter the encryption password:

    `stepnine`

    This sets the program to working. Again, if you forget this password, you will not be able to access this file.

6.  Select *OK* to acknowledge the completion of decryption.

Quit DISKREET again by selecting *Quit!* from the menu bar. Now reexamine TESTFILE. It should have returned to its original state and you should see the text you entered earlier. (TESTFILE.SEC is destroyed in the process of decryption.)

- *Figure 9.2: The contents of TESTFILE encrypted*

# ENCRYPTED DRIVES (NDISKS)

In this part of the tutorial, you will create an NDisk, or encrypted drive. An NDisk acts like any other drive on your system: it has a drive letter, it can have files copied to and from it, and it can have subdirectories. An NDisk differs from other drives, however, in several ways. You must, of course, have a password to access it. Moreover, an NDisk is not a physical drive, but a logical drive, which is actually a chunk of space set aside on your hard disk. And finally, any file copied to an NDisk is automatically encrypted. This prevents more sophisticated snoops from looking directly at the data on the disk.

To create an NDisk, do the following:

1. Restart DISKREET.

2. Select the *Disks* option on the first dialog box.

3. When asked if you wish to define a new Diskreet drive (NDisk), select *No*. (You will only be asked if no NDisks currently exist.) The Diskreet Disks screen, shown in Figure 9.3, appears.

4. Select the *Make* option at the bottom of the Diskreet Disks screen.

5. From the drive list that appears, select *C:*, the drive whose space the NDisk will use and select *OK*.

6. At the *File name:* prompt on the next dialog box, type

   **step9**

   This names the NDisk you are creating. Any legal DOS file name is legal here. Do not, however, use a file extension (e.g., STEP9.DSK).

7. Select *OK*.

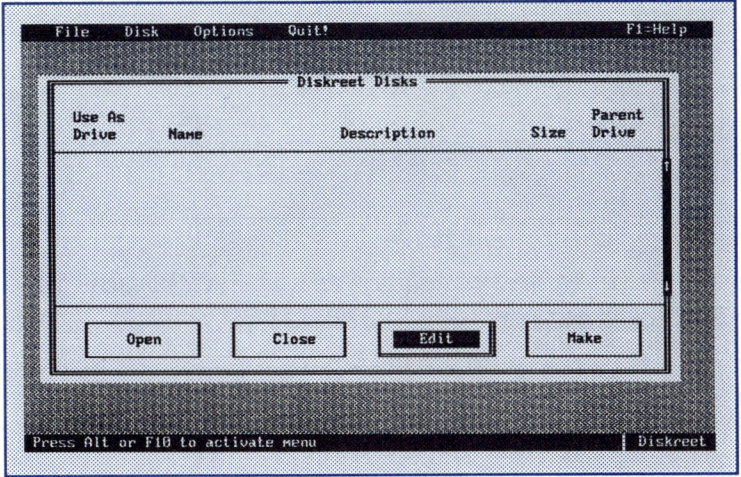

■ *Figure 9.3: The Diskreet Disks screen with no NDisks*

8.  On the next dialog box, you must specify the size of the NDisk. That is, you must choose how much space on drive C you wish to reserve for the NDisk. Select the *Specific size* radio button and enter

    **1000**

    at the corresponding prompt. This will create an NDisk one megabyte in size.

9.  Select *OK*.

10. Now enter the password you wish to use to access the NDisk. The password must be at least six characters long. Type

    **heliotrope**

    and press Enter.

11. Reenter the password. Again, this is to make certain you assigned the password you intended to assign. *Do not forget this password! You will not be able to access your NDisk if you do!*

12. Select *OK* to acknowledge the warning about forgetting a password.

13. Select a drive letter for the NDisk and select *OK*. There should only be one choice: the next letter in sequence. That is, if you have two floppies (A and B) and one hard disk with one partition (C), the NDisk will be drive D.

14. Press any key to acknowledge audit information. This information is displayed every time you open the NDisk. The new drive should appear on the Diskreet Disks screen, as in Figure 9.4.

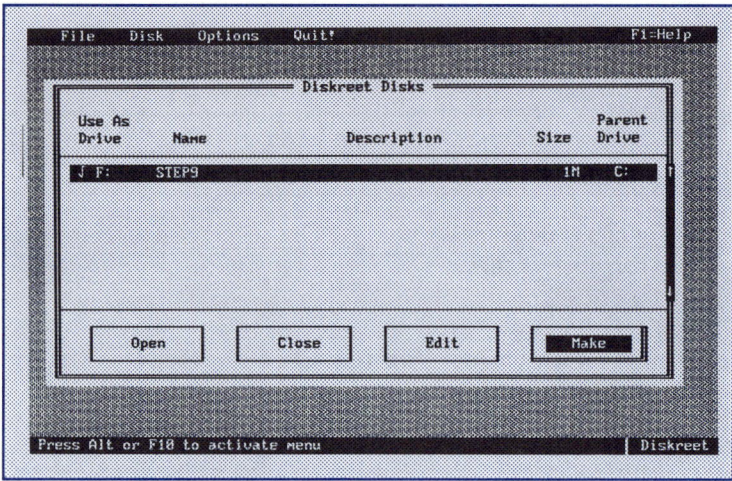

■ *Figure 9.4: The new NDisk*

15. Select the *Close* option and quit DISKREET by selecting *Quit!* from the menu bar.

You have created an encrypted drive.

## OPENING AN NDISK

To access an NDisk, it must be opened. Opening an NDisk is quite simple—just address the drive (by copying a file to it or changing to that drive) and supply the password.

Do this now by changing to the drive. Enter

    D:

or the proper drive letter for the NDisk.

Enter the password to open the drive. When you have done this, change back to your hard disk by entering

    C:

Once an NDisk is open, it will remain open until you close it. You close an open NDisk by pressing both Shift keys simultaneously.

You may change this key combination to some other combination of the Shift, Ctrl, and Alt keys. To do this, use the *Keyboard and screen lock...* option on the Options pull-down menu in the DISKREET program.

Of course, once an NDisk is closed, you must reopen it to use it again.

# DELETING NDISKS

If you wish to keep the NDisk you have created and experiment with it for a while, you may end the exercise right now. If, however, you would like to delete it, or any other NDisk, do the following:

1. Close all open NDisks by pressing both Shift keys. You cannot delete an open NDisk.

2. Start DISKREET.

3. Highlight the NDisk to delete (there is only one and it should already be highlighted).

4. Pull down the Disk menu and select the *Delete...* option.

5. When prompted for the main password, press Enter. The main password is a DISKREET program password that is different from the password you assigned to the NDisk. By default it is set to Enter and will remain so unless you change it.

6. Select the Delete option at the confirmation box. The NDisk should be removed from the Diskreet Disks screen.

7. Quit DISKREET.

# *Monitoring Disk Access*

DISKMON (Disk Monitor), a small (8K) memory-resident program, has three functions. The first, and the only one of the three that is really relevant to data security, write-protects your disks so that you are prompted for confirmation every time a program tries to modify or delete a protected area or file. This can prevent the accidental deletion of important files.

The second function provides a drive activity light on your screen. Whenever a disk is accessed, the drive letter flashes in the upper right corner of the screen. As this light works just like the lights on your floppy disk drives and hard disk, it is most useful for monitoring network drives and RAM drives, or for people who work with their computer on the floor.

*Drive activity light*

The third and final function parks the heads on your hard disk. This is a safeguard for your data. When subject to extreme physical stresses, the read/write heads can crash into the surface of the disk (head-crash). If the heads crash into a part of the disk containing data, the data may be destroyed. Parking the disks moves

*Parking hard disk heads*

**69**

the heads away from areas that contain data. Most hard disks sold these days park automatically when power is turned off, but some do not.

This step contains a brief tutorial on the first of these three functions. The other two functions will also be briefly discussed. You should be able to work through this step in about 15 minutes.

## WRITE-PROTECTING YOUR DISKS

In this tutorial, you will configure DISKMON to prompt you for confirmation whenever you try to delete or modify a file.

1.  Start the DISKMON program by entering

    `diskmon`

    at the command line or by selecting the *Disk Monitor* option under the SECURITY topic in the Norton Utilities Shell.

2.  When the program starts, select the *Disk Protect* option from the main program screen. This brings up the screen shown in Figure 10.1.

3.  Select the *Files* radio button. This instructs DISKMON to write-protect the files on your machine listed in the Files box.

4.  In the Files box, change *.COM to read *.*. This causes all files to be protected.

5.  Select the *ON* option at the bottom of the dialog box. This saves the configuration you entered (all future DISKMON sessions will have this configuration unless you change it again), loads DISKMON into memory, and activates it.

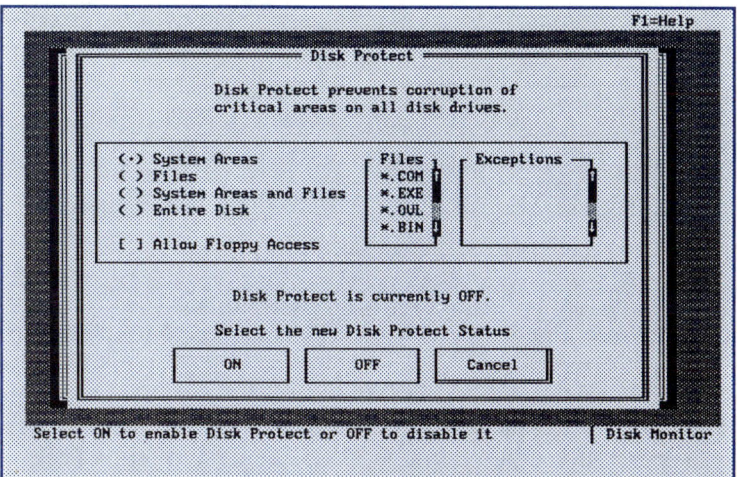

■ *Figure 10.1: DISKMON's Write-Protection options*

Although we only write-protected files in the previous exercise,
you may have noticed that the screen shown in Figure 10.1 displays several other options. These act as follows:

■ *System Areas:* Write-protects essential system information,
such as the partition table and boot record. This is a useful
option since viruses can attack these areas of your disk.

■ *Files:* Write-protects all files listed in the Files box. Any
files listed in the Exceptions box will not be protected.

■ *System Areas and Files:* Combines the above two options.

■ *Entire Disk:* Protects absolutely everything on every
drive—system area, files, and empty space. This option is
more a hindrance than a help, however. Something as
simple as copying a 500-byte file produces multiple
prompts for confirmation.

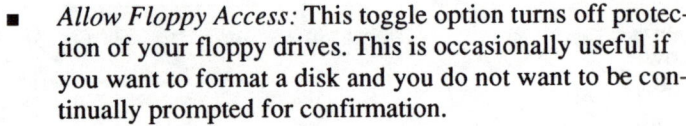

■ *Allow Floppy Access:* This toggle option turns off protection of your floppy drives. This is occasionally useful if you want to format a disk and you do not want to be continually prompted for confirmation.

Now quit DISKMON and test the write protection by attempting to delete the DISKMON program from your disk. Type

```
del c:\norton\diskmon.exe
```

A confirmation box warning you that a deletion is being attempted appears (see Figure 10.2). Be careful here. Type **N** to prevent the DISKMON program file from being deleted. Typing **Y** allows the file to be deleted. Typing **D** (for *Disable Protection*) allows the file to be deleted and turns DISKMON off, thereby disabling write protection. If you turn DISKMON off and wish to turn it back on, simply restart the program and select the *ON* option from the screen shown in Figure 10.1.

You may decide that you like the idea of having write protection on at all times. Though you can enable write protection once a session with the *ON* option shown in Figure 10.1, it is easier to load and activate the program from your AUTOEXEC.BAT file. Simply add the command

```
diskmon /protect+
```

near the end of your AUTOEXEC.BAT file and DISKMON will be loaded and activated every time you start your machine.

## ACTIVATING THE DISK LIGHT

If you like the idea of seeing a disk activity light on your screen, either because you are a frequent user of network drives or because you keep your computer on the floor, you can do the following:

1. Start DISKMON.

2. Select the *Disk Light* option from the main screen.

3. Select *ON*.

If the light is on, selecting *OFF* in step 3 deactivates it.

## PARKING YOUR HARD DISK

If you have an older model hard disk whose heads do not automatically park when the power is turned off, it is a good idea to park the drive heads yourself. This prevents data loss in the event of a hard disk head crash. To park the drive heads, the *last* thing you should do before shutting off power to your machine is

1. Start DISKMON.

2. Select the *Disk Park* option from the program's main screen.

```
C:\ del c:\norton\diskmon.exe
─────────────────── Disk Monitor ───────────────────
│ A delete operation was attempted on a protected file. │
│       Do you wish to allow this operation?            │
│       Yes        No        Disable Protection         │
```

■ *Figure 10.2: The Write-Protection confirmation box*

# *Destroying Data*

■ ■ ■ ■ ■ ■ ■ ■ ■ ■ ■

Occasionally it becomes necessary, for reasons of security, to dispose of data in some permanent way. As you saw in Step 4 of this book, simply erasing files is insufficient because it does not actually delete data from your disks; erased files can be easily unerased. The WIPEINFO program, by contrast, disposes of data by overwriting files or entire disks.

Because WIPEINFO actually replaces your files with new and meaningless data, it is impossible to recover your files once they have been "wiped." You must be very sure, therefore, that you no longer need or want the files or disks you are going to wipe.

This step contains a tutorial on the WIPEINFO program. You will learn how to wipe both individual files and entire disks. It should take you about 15 minutes to complete.

# WIPING FILES

Before we actually begin the tutorial, create three short sample files with your word processor. Save them on a blank floppy disk in your A drive and give them the names FILE1.TXT, FILE2.TXT, FILE3.DOC.

Do not use one of your regular data disks or any disk that holds data that you need. In the second half of this tutorial, the entire disk will be wiped.

Once your sample disk is prepared, you are ready to start. With your sample disk in drive A:

1.  Start WIPEINFO by entering

    `wipeinfo`

    at the command line or by selecting the *WipeInfo* option under the SECURITY topic in the Norton Utilities Shell.

2.  On the program's main screen, select the *Files* option. This brings up the Wipe Files screen, shown in Figure 11.1.

3.  At the prompt at the top of the File Name box, specify the name of the file(s) to delete, making sure to include a drive letter and path. Delete the first two sample files by typing

    `a:*.txt`

    (For those of you who are not familiar with wildcards in file names, this command means "delete all files on drive A with the extension TXT.")

4.  Make sure that the *Confirm each file* option is toggled on. Enabling this option causes WIPEINFO to prompt you before wiping each file.

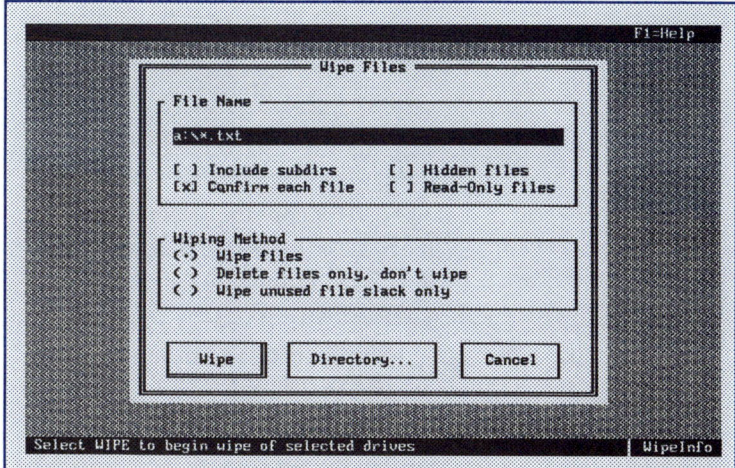

F1=Help

■ *Figure 11.1: WIPEINFO's Wipe Files screen*

There are three other options for wiping files that won't be used in this exercise. Their functions are listed below:

■ *Hidden files:* Causes WIPEINFO to wipe any hidden files specified. WIPEINFO does not wipe hidden files if this option is off.

■ *Read-Only files:* Causes WIPEINFO to wipe any read-only files specified. WIPEINFO does not wipe read-only files if this option is off.

■ *Include subdirs:* Causes WIPEINFO to wipe the specified file(s) in the specified directory and all of its sub-directories. (In the current example, all files with the extension .TXT would be wiped from A:\ and all subdirectories of A:\)

*Wipe Files options*

To continue:

5.  In the Wiping Method box, select the *Wipe files* radio button.

6.  Select the *Wipe* option at the bottom of the dialog box to start the wiping procedure.

7.  On the warning dialog box that appears, select the *Wipe* option. This brings up the screen shown in Figure 11.2, where you are prompted for confirmation before each file is wiped.

8.  Select the *Wipe* option twice—once to confirm the wiping of FILE1.TXT and once to confirm FILE2.TXT.

*Con-firmation screen options*

There are three other options on the confirmation screen shown in Figure 11.2. They are described in the list below:

■   *Skip:* Does not wipe the highlighted file.

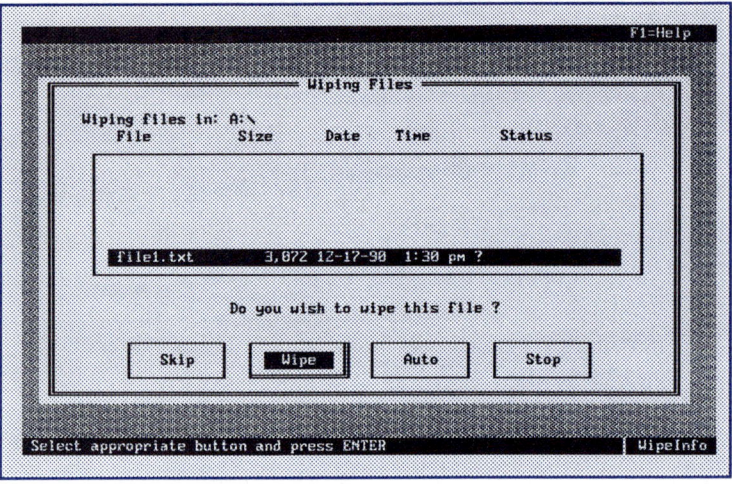

■ *Figure 11.2: WIPEINFO's confirmation screen*

- *Wipe:* Wipes the highlighted file.

- *Auto:* Wipes the current file and all subsequent files.

- *Stop:* Quits and returns you to WIPEINFO's main screen.

When the two files have been wiped, select *OK* to acknowledge completion and return to WIPEINFO's main screen.

## WIPING ENTIRE DISKS

WIPEINFO can wipe the contents of entire disks in addition to wiping individual files. In the second half of this tutorial, you will wipe the contents of the sample disk in drive A.

1. The first half of the tutorial should have left you at WIPEINFO's main screen. Select the *Drives* option.

2. In the Drives box on the screen that appears, toggle on *A:,* the drive you wish to wipe. Note that you can wipe multiple drives at once by toggling multiple drives here.

3. On the same screen, in the Wiping Method box, make sure that the *Wipe entire drive* radio button is selected. (The *Wipe unused areas only* radio button causes WIPEINFO to wipe only the empty space on the selected drives and leave any files alone. This can be useful if you previously deleted some files with the DOS DEL command that you now wish to wipe.)

4. Select the *Wipe* option at the bottom of the dialog box.

5. Select the *Wipe* option on the warning dialog box. This sets WIPEINFO to wiping the sample disk.

6. When wiping is done, select *OK* to acknowledge completion and return to WIPEINFO's main screen.

To check that WIPEINFO works as advertised, use the UNERASE program to try and unerase the sample files from the sample disk in drive A. First, quit WIPEINFO by selecting the *Quit* option on the main screen. At the DOS prompt, type

`unerase a:`

which will start UNERASE working on drive A. The

`No files found`

message tells you that the sample files are gone and cannot be unerased. Quit UNERASE by selecting *Quit!* from the menu bar.

## CONFIGURING WIPEINFO

You may have noticed a fourth option on the WIPEINFO main screen called *Configure*. This option lets you change the way WIPEINFO overwrites data when it is wiping. Selecting *Configure* presents you with the following three options:

- *Fast Wipe:* This radio button (the default selection) allows you to specify the character WIPEINFO uses to overwrite files or disk. The default value is 0 and there is no reason to change this.

- *Government Wipe:* This radio button allows you to wipe data according to Department of Defense specifications. This involves multiple overwrites with different characters.

- *Repeat Count:* Allows you to specify the number of times to overwrite the specified files or drives. The default is 1 and there really isn't any reason to change this.

If you should decide to change any of the configuration options, select the *Save settings* option to make your changes permanent.

# Viewing and Editing Data

DISKEDIT is probably the most powerful program in the Norton Utilities. It allows you to view or edit data *anywhere* on your disk. Not only can you change or simply examine data in files that are not normally accessible, such as program files, you also have access to data in unoccupied (i.e., erased) disk space and data in critical areas of your hard disk: the File Allocation Tables (FATs), partition tables, and more.

Because DISKEDIT is so powerful, it is also potentially dangerous. Making even the smallest erroneous changes to critical areas of your hard disk can result in massive data loss.

Do not let this discourage you from proceeding, however. This step contains a brief tour of some of the basic features and capabilities of DISKEDIT. It should take you about 30 minutes to complete and absorb. We will work in read-only mode at all times, thereby preventing any modifications, accidental or otherwise, to your disk or data.

**STEP**

**12**

# STARTING DISKEDIT

Let's begin the tour by starting the DISKEDIT program.

1. Enter

   **diskedit**

   at the command line or

   **de**

   if you changed the program name during installation. Alternatively, you can select the *Disk Editor* option under the RECOVERY topic in the Norton Utilities Shell.

*Read-only mode* When the program starts, a dialog box will tell you that you are working in read-only mode and that you cannot, therefore, make changes to your data. (For future reference, read-only mode can be turned off as follows: Pull down the Tools menu and select the *cOnfiguration* option. On the dialog box that appears, toggle off the *Read Only* option and then select *Save*.)

2. Select *OK* to acknowledge the dialog box.

After the program reads your disk, you will see the structure of the current directory. Figure 12.1 happens to show the directory in which the Norton Utilities are located. You will see some familiar and some unfamiliar information. The file name, extension, size, date, and time are all part of a standard directory listing obtained with the DOS DIR command. However, the numbers in the column marked Cluster, which show the location of a file's starting point on the disk, may be unfamiliar to many users, as may the meaning of the file's attributes. Moreover, if you scroll down, you may see the names of erased files that you used to have in this directory. These are distinguished by the sigma character (σ) at the beginning of their names.

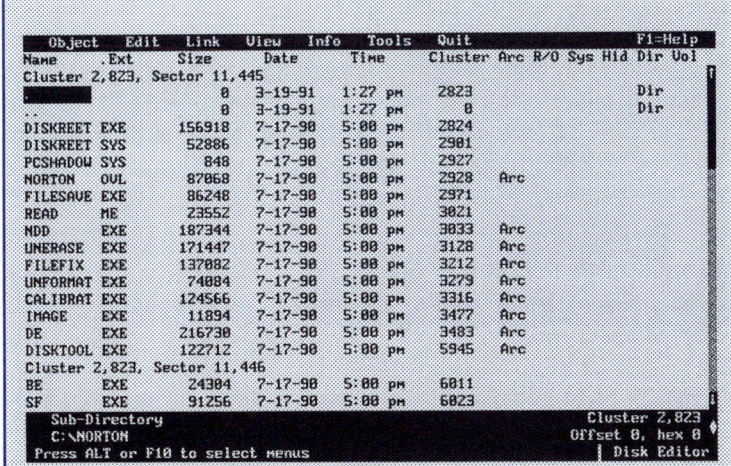

| Object | Edit | Link | View | Info | Tools | Quit | | | | | | F1=Help |
|--------|------|------|------|------|-------|------|------|------|------|------|------|---------|
| Name | .Ext | Size | Date | Time | | Cluster | Arc | R/O | Sys | Hid | Dir | Vol |
| Cluster 2,823, Sector 11,445 | | | | | | | | | | | | |
| ▮ | | 0 | 3-19-91 | 1:27 pm | | 2823 | | | | | Dir | |
| .. | | 0 | 3-19-91 | 1:27 pm | | 0 | | | | | Dir | |
| DISKREET | EXE | 156918 | 7-17-90 | 5:00 pm | | 2824 | | | | | | |
| DISKREET | SYS | 52886 | 7-17-90 | 5:00 pm | | 2901 | | | | | | |
| PCSHADOW | SYS | 848 | 7-17-90 | 5:00 pm | | 2927 | | | | | | |
| NORTON | OVL | 87068 | 7-17-90 | 5:00 pm | | 2928 | Arc | | | | | |
| FILESAVE | EXE | 86248 | 7-17-90 | 5:00 pm | | 2971 | | | | | | |
| READ | ME | 23552 | 7-17-90 | 5:00 pm | | 3021 | | | | | | |
| NDD | EXE | 187344 | 7-17-90 | 5:00 pm | | 3033 | Arc | | | | | |
| UNERASE | EXE | 171447 | 7-17-90 | 5:00 pm | | 3128 | Arc | | | | | |
| FILEFIX | EXE | 137082 | 7-17-90 | 5:00 pm | | 3212 | Arc | | | | | |
| UNFORMAT | EXE | 74084 | 7-17-90 | 5:00 pm | | 3279 | Arc | | | | | |
| CALIBRAT | EXE | 124566 | 7-17-90 | 5:00 pm | | 3316 | Arc | | | | | |
| IMAGE | EXE | 11894 | 7-17-90 | 5:00 pm | | 3477 | Arc | | | | | |
| DE | EXE | 216730 | 7-17-90 | 5:00 pm | | 3483 | Arc | | | | | |
| DISKTOOL | EXE | 122712 | 7-17-90 | 5:00 pm | | 5945 | Arc | | | | | |
| Cluster 2,823, Sector 11,446 | | | | | | | | | | | | |
| BE | EXE | 24304 | 7-17-90 | 5:00 pm | | 6011 | | | | | | |
| SF | EXE | 91256 | 7-17-90 | 5:00 pm | | 6023 | | | | | | |

```
 Sub-Directory                                     Cluster 2,823
 C:\NORTON                                          Offset 0, hex 0
 Press ALT or F10 to select menus              │ Disk Editor
```

▪ *Figure 12.1: The Norton Utilities directory*

Were we making any changes, editing this directory would be as simple as moving the highlight bar to the desired location (with either the arrow keys or the mouse) and entering the edits we want.

# FATS

The *File Allocation Table,* or FAT, is the means by which DOS keeps track of all of the files on a disk. Through the FAT, DOS tracks every single cluster, whether it is free, whether it is in use and if so, by what file, and whether it has been marked as bad and taken out of use.

To bring the FAT, shown in Figure 12.2, into view, pull down the Object menu and select the *1st copy of FAT* option. Each position on the screen represents one cluster on your hard disk. Move the highlight bar around and watch the lower left corner of your screen. The name of the file to which the highlighted cluster belongs, if any, will be displayed. Any other clusters belonging to that file will also be marked; these are usually adjacent to the highlighted position. The position highlighted in Figure 12.2, for example, along with the positions numbered 4–12, belong to IO.SYS, one of the system files that causes your machine to boot. Notice that some positions are marked

**<EOF>**

This means that the cluster in question is the last in a file or is the "End of File" cluster. Other positions are marked with a 0. These clusters are unused.

If you were to edit the FAT and mark clusters incorrectly, DOS would no longer be able to find any of the corresponding files and you would lose them all. You can see, then, why DISKEDIT is so

```
  Object   Edit   Link   View   Info   Tools   Quit                    F1=Help
Sector 1
         9       10      11       12    <EOF>       14       15       16
        17       18      19       20       21       22       23       24
        25       26      27    <EOF>     6380       30       31    <EOF>
        33       34      35       45    <EOF>       39       84       40
     <EOF>     5810   <EOF>    <EOF>       94    <EOF>    <EOF>       48
        51       50      85       52       53       54       55       56
     <EOF>       58      59       60       61    <EOF>       63       64
        65       66      67       68       70    <EOF>       71       72
        73    <EOF>      75    <EOF>       77       78       79       80
        82    <EOF>      83      105      741    <EOF>       87       89
       739       91    6673       92       93       96      123     6624
        97      126   12252      100      101      102      114    <EOF>
     <EOF>      106     107      108      109      110      111      112
       113      732     115      118      117    <EOF>      119      120
       121      122     124     3433      125      755      127      128
       129      130     131      132    <EOF>     1193     1194        0
         0      138   <EOF>        0    <EOF>    <EOF>    <EOF>    <EOF>
       145      146   <EOF>      148    <EOF>    <EOF>      151    <EOF>
     <EOF>      154   <EOF>      156      157      158      159      160
  FAT (1st Copy)                                               Sector 1
  C:\IO.SYS                                              Cluster 2, hex 2
  Press ALT or F10 to select menus                        | Disk Editor
```

■ *Figure 12.2: A File Allocation Table*

potentially dangerous. Unless you know exactly what you are doing, editing a FAT is a good recipe for disaster.

# FILES

DISKEDIT can look into (and edit) files as easily as it can look into critical areas of your hard disk. Keep in mind, however, that DISKEDIT is not a text editor, and it couldn't easily be used as such. It is a rather different tool as it can view (or edit) .EXE files, .COM files, or any file for that matter. For example, to view the files comprising the UNERASE programs, perform the following actions:

1.  Pull down the Object menu and select the *File...* option.

2.  At the *File name:* prompt on the dialog box that appears, type

    `c:\norton\unerase.exe`

    and then select *OK*.

Your screen should be divided into three parts, as in Figure 12.3. What you see here is the beginning of a file that contains very little text and a great deal of compiled code.

The left side of the screen displays the line numbers. Like any text file, a program file is divided into lines of characters. Notice, however, that these lines are numbered in hexadecimal rather than decimal notation (in numbers base 16 rather than base 10). This is simply a different system of counting. In decimal notation (regular numbers) we count from 0 to 9 and then go to 10, we count from 10 to 19 and go to 20, and so on. In hexadecimal notation, we count from 0 to F (i.e., ...8, 9, A, B, C, D, E, F) and then go to 10, we count from 10 to 1F (i.e., ...18, 19, 1A, 1B ...) and go to 20, and so on.

*Line numbers*

**Hex code**

Occupying the large, center portion of the screen is the listing of the program, which, like the program line numbers, is given in hexadecimal.

**ASCII code**

The right side of the screen displays the ASCII characters equivalent to the hex characters shown in the center portion of the screen. If "garbage" of this sort looks familiar, that's because it is exactly what you get if you try to look at the contents of a program file or some other nontext or nondocument file using the DOS TYPE command.

While this kind of garbage is meaningless to all but the most experienced eyes, many program files do have some coherent text embedded in them. You can use DISKEDIT to view such text—error messages, menu or option names, copyright notices, and so on—usually anything a program types out as text on your screen.

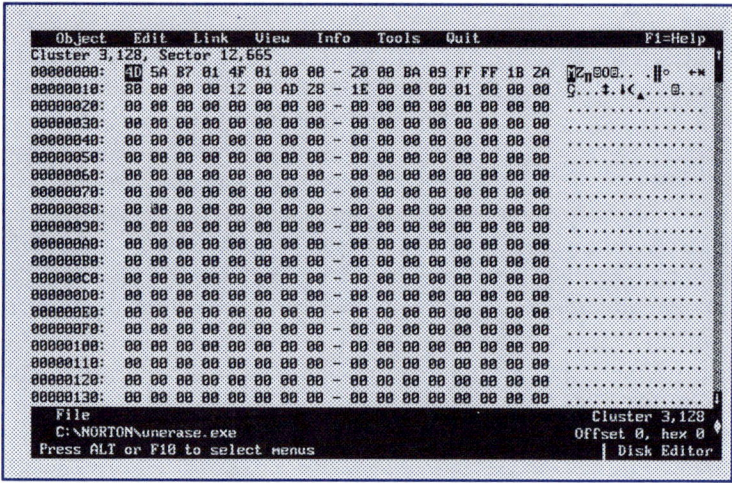

■ *Figure 12.3: DISKEDIT's view of UNERASE.EXE*

For example, let's use DISKEDIT to search for Peter Norton's copyright notice in the UNERASE program.

1.  Pull down the Tools menu and select the *Find...* option.

2.  At the ASCII prompt on the dialog box that appears, type

    (C)

    and select the *Find* option.

DISKEDIT should find the copyright notice quickly. The results are displayed on your screen as follows:

**(C) Copyright 1984-89 by Peter Norton**

Take a few minutes to use the PgUp and PgDn keys or the *Find...* command again to find some other text within UNERASE. You will notice as you move about that there are two highlight bars, one in the hex listing and one in the ASCII listing. They work, in effect, as one highlight bar, because the characters they show are equivalent to each other.

Were we making changes to UNERASE (i.e., if DISKEDIT's read-only status were turned off), you could edit the file simply by making changes at the highlight bar. However, if you are not an expert, it is not a good idea to edit files with DISKEDIT. Indiscriminate changes made to any program file may prevent the program from executing properly.

## VIEWING DATA ON YOUR DISK

As you saw in Step 5 on the UNERASE program, when you delete a file, its data remains on the disk even as the space it occupies is made available again for new files. It is possible with DISKEDIT to view data on your disk that is no longer part of a file.

1. Pull down the Object menu and select the *Cluster...* option.

2. At the *Starting Cluster:* prompt on the dialog box that appears, enter a large number close to the largest cluster number shown and select *OK*.

You will see a screen much like the one you saw while viewing UNERASE. Look in the lower left corner of the screen. If a file name (complete with path) appears there, it means that the cluster you selected is part of the named file. Repeat step 2 until you find one that is not in use. Unused clusters will be marked with an *Unused cluster* message in place of a file name. You may recognize some of your old data in the unused cluster you find.

## QUITTING DISKEDIT

Though we did not exercise any of DISKEDIT's editing functions, we did take a close look at the data on your hard disk. Feel free to look around a bit more, but if you've had enough, you can quit DISKEDIT by pressing Ctrl-Q.

# *Finding Files*

Hard disks are getting larger and larger. The number of files you are able to keep grows proportionately. Consequently, it is getting easier to misplace a file that you need. One of the most useful of the Norton Utilities is the FILEFIND program, which, as its name implies, can find a file or files anywhere on your hard disk.

This step consists of a tutorial that will take you through the more common uses of FILEFIND. It should take you about 30 minutes to complete.

## CREATING SAMPLE FILES

Before the tutorial actually begins, use your word processor to create two sample files to find. Make sure to save these files in ASCII format. This will enable you to view them easily later on in the exercise. In the first, type

```
This is the first sample file used in Step 13.
```

and save it under the name C:\STEP13.1. In the second, type

```
This is the second sample file used in
Step 13.
```

and save it under the name C:\NORTON\STEP13.2. Make sure to include the path along with the file name. This will ensure that the files are "lost" in a few different directories on your hard disk.

## FINDING FILES

Now that a few files are conveniently lost, we will begin the tutorial by finding them again.

1.  Start the FILEFIND program by entering

    ```
    filefind
    ```

    at the command line or

    ```
    ff
    ```

    if you renamed the program during installation. Alternatively, you can select the *File Find* option under the TOOLS topic in the Norton Utilities Shell. When the program starts, the dialog box shown in Figure 13.1 appears.

2.  At the *File Name:* prompt at the top of this dialog box, type

    ```
    step13.*
    ```

    This instructs FILEFIND to search for every file with the name STEP13 and, effectively, to ignore the file extension. It will find, therefore, any of the files with names listed below:

    ■   STEP13.1

    ■   STEP13.2

    ■   STEP13.BAK

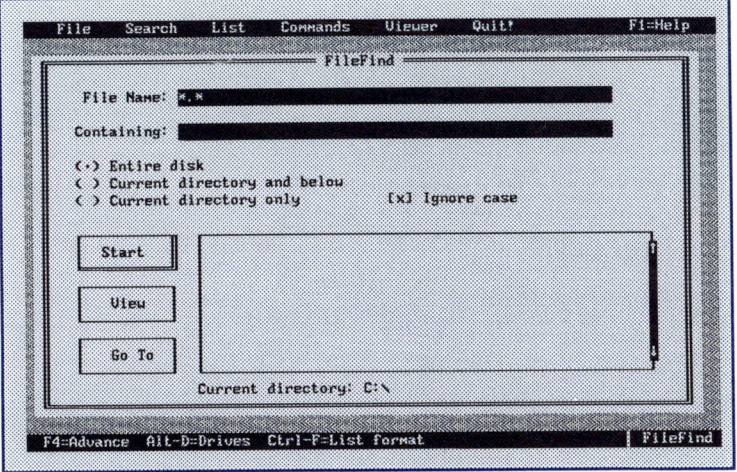

```
   File   Search   List   Commands   Viewer   Quit?                    F1=Help
┌──────────────────────────── FileFind ──────────────────────────────┐
│                                                                     │
│   File Name: *.*                                                    │
│                                                                     │
│   Containing:                                                       │
│                                                                     │
│   (•) Entire disk                                                   │
│   ( ) Current directory and below                                   │
│   ( ) Current directory only          [x] Ignore case               │
│                                                                     │
│   ┌─────────┐   ┌────────────────────────────────────────┐         │
│   │  Start  │   │                                          ▲         │
│   └─────────┘   │                                                    │
│   ┌─────────┐   │                                                    │
│   │  View   │   │                                                    │
│   └─────────┘   │                                                    │
│   ┌─────────┐   │                                                    │
│   │  Go To  │   │                                          ▼         │
│   └─────────┘   └────────────────────────────────────────┘         │
│                                                                     │
│             Current directory:  C:\                                 │
│                                                                     │
 F4=Advance  Alt-D=Drives  Ctrl-F=List format              │ FileFind │
```

■ *Figure 13.1: The FILEFIND main dialog box*

■ STEP13.MOM

■ STEP13

3. Select the *Entire disk* radio button. This causes FILEFIND to search all of, rather than selected parts of, your hard disk.

4. Select the *Start* option to begin the search.

5. When the search is finished, select *OK* to acknowledge completion. Any files found matching the search criteria given in step 2 above are displayed in the list box, as in Figure 13.2. STEP13.1 was found in the root directory (C:\) and STEP13.2 was found in the \NORTON directory, just where we lost them.

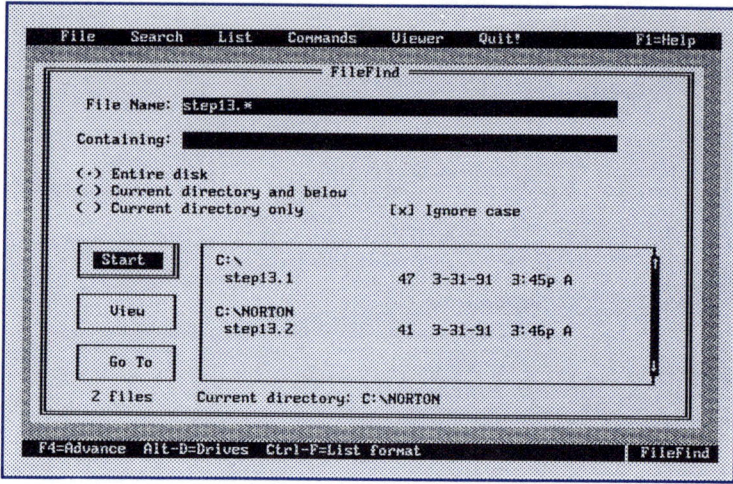

■ *Figure 13.2: The results of a search*

# VIEWING FOUND FILES

When searching for files under less contrived conditions, it helps to be able to view the files you have found. Often, more than two files will appear in the list box; some will be the ones you are seeking, and others not. To view one of the sample files you have just found:

1.  Press the → key to move the highlight bar into the list box.

2.  Use the ↑ or ↓ key to highlight STEP13.1.

3.  Select the *View* option. The contents of the highlighted file are then displayed, as in Figure 13.3. If the file you are viewing is larger than can be displayed on one screen, you can view the balance of the file by scrolling downward.

4.  Select the *Main!* option on the menu bar to return to the main dialog box.

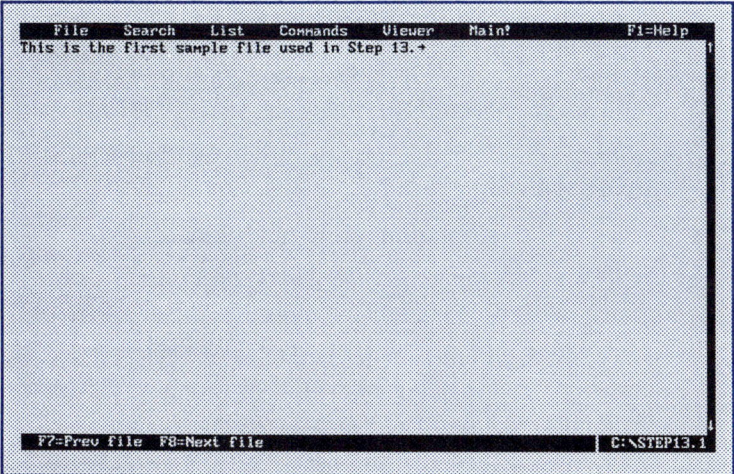

- *Figure 13.3: Viewing a Found File*

# SEARCHING FOR TEXT

There may be times when you can't remember the name of a file
but you do know what is in it. Perhaps someone else created it for
you or perhaps it just slipped your mind. You will not be able to
find the file using the search detailed in the previous exercise if
you don't know its name. Fortunately, FILEFIND can search for
files not only by looking for file names, but also by looking for a
particular string of text within a file. Users of version 4.5 will recognize this function as the TS (Text Search) program.

To search for a file or files by searching for a particular text string,
do the following:

1.  At the *File Name:* prompt at the top of the main dialog
    box, type

    *.*

This will cause FILEFIND to search through every file on the specified disk. (If, however, you know that you are looking for a Lotus 1-2-3 file, you could enter **\*.wk1**, or, for a Microsoft Word file, **\*.doc**, etc.)

2. At the *Containing:* prompt, type the text you wish to search for. For the purposes of this tutorial, type

   `This is the second sample file.`

3. Make sure the *Entire disk* radio button is selected so as to search your entire hard disk.

4. Select the *Start* option to begin the search. The search may take a while, depending on the size of your hard disk and the number of files that must be scanned.

5. When the search is finished, select *OK* to acknowlege completion. Again, the files found will be listed in the list box. This search should have found the file STEP13.1.

You can view the contents of the found files by following the steps outlined under "Viewing Files" above.

## CHANGING FILE ATTRIBUTES

All DOS files can have as many as four properties, or attributes, which cause them to act in different ways. These four attributes, and the properties they impart upon files, are listed below:

■ System: Makes a disk bootable. Applies only to the DOS system files (IO.SYS and MSDOS.SYS in MS-DOS, IBOBIO.COM and IBMDOS.COM in PC-DOS).

■ Hidden: Causes a file not to be displayed in the normal directory listing displayed by the DOS DIR command.

■ Read-only: Files with this attribute set cannot be altered or deleted.

- Archive: Allows files to be backed up with the DOS BACKUP program.

Occasionally it will be necessary for you to modify a file's attributes. Perhaps you have an important file on a machine used by others. Marking it as read-only will prevent it from being deleted. Or, if you wish to hide a file for an added measure of security, you can mark a file as hidden. You can turn a file's attributes on or off by following the steps below, substituting the appropriate option for *Read Only* as necessary:

1. In the list box, highlight the file whose attributes you wish to change (STEP13.2 for the purposes of this exercise).

2. Pull down the Commands menu and select the *set Attributes...* option.

3. Make the file read-only by toggling on the *Read Only* option in the Set column of the dialog box that appears.

4. Select *OK* to set the new attribute.

5. Select *OK* again to acknowledge completion of the operation.

To check your results, quit FILEFIND by selecting *Quit!* on the menu bar. Now try to delete the file by entering

```
del c:\norton\step13.2
```

at the command line. You should see the message *Access denied,* meaning that the file cannot be deleted.

This brings you to the end of the FILEFIND tutorial. Close up shop by deleting the two sample files. Remember, however, that in order to delete STEP13.2, you must first go back into FILEFIND, search for the file, and clear the read-only attribute. (Follow the instructions above, but this time toggle on the *Read Only* option in the Clear column rather than in the Set column.)

# *Basic System Configuration*

The value of the Norton Utilities lies in their ability to do all those things that DOS doesn't do (or doesn't do well). This is most apparent when you use them to accomplish big things, like unerasing files and unformatting disks; however, the Norton Utilities can also do some little things that, while not as spectacular as recovering lost data, are quite worthwhile.

The Norton Control Center (NCC) program is a collection of ten of these little things. NCC allows you to change the size of your cursor; change screen colors and the number of lines on your screen; adjust the sensitivity of your keyboard and mouse; set serial port configuration; set the system date and time; use date, time, and currency settings for different countries; and use stopwatches.

This step provides an overview of each of the NCC functions. Take 15 minutes or so to explore these functions; they could be valuable to you.

# STARTING THE PROGRAM

To start the program, enter

**ncc**

from the DOS command line or select the *Control Center* option under the TOOLS topic in the Norton Utilities Shell. This produces the screen shown in Figure 14.1.

This screen is divided into two parts, as are all NCC screens. The Select Item box, on the left, contains the ten NCC functions; the right two-thirds of the screen shows a different dialog box for whichever function is currently selected.

*Navigating NCC*

Using NCC requires that you move back and forth between the two screen halves. First you select a function in the Select Item

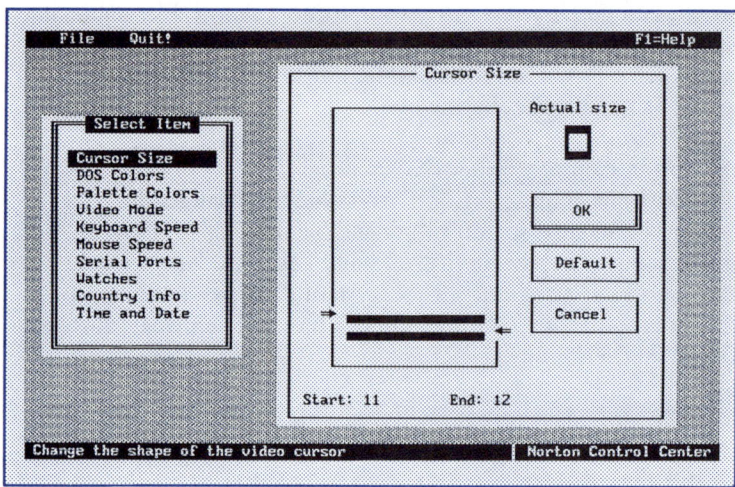

■ *Figure 14.1: The NCC Cursor Size screen*

box by highlighting the one you want and pressing Enter or the appropriate key. This activates the corresponding dialog box on the right. When you have chosen the options you want, selecting *OK* or pressing Enter moves you back to the Select Item box. Quitting NCC activates the changes you have made.

## SETTING CURSOR SIZE

Some users, especially laptop users, find the standard DOS cursor too small and difficult to see. If you are among these users, you may prefer a larger cursor, or one that does not sit at the bottom of the line. Selecting the *Cursor Size* option produces a dialog box on which you can adjust the size of your cursor.

Move the Start and End arrows up and down until the cursor is sized as you like it. You can drag the arrows with the mouse, or you can highlight them and then use the ↑ and ↓ keys. The cursor you create by moving these arrows can be seen in the box marked *Actual size*. When you are adjusting cursor size, keep in mind the following points:

- The *Default* option sets the cursor size back to the DOS default, so don't be afraid to experiment.

- Make sure that the Start arrow is above the End arrow. If not, the cursor may disappear altogether.

## CHANGING TEXT COLORS

White text on a black background is boring. Selecting the *DOS Colors* option allows you to change the color of the text, the background, and the screen border.

On the color list in the Text Color box, move the selection arrows to the color combination you want. All available combinations of text and background colors are accessible here. There is a small sample of text that shows you what your selection will look like. To set your border, select the color you want from the list of colors in the Border Color box.

The Default option restores colors to white on black with a black border.

## CHANGING THE COLOR PALETTE

EGA and VGA monitors can display (at least) 64 colors. However, you can access only 16 of them at once. If you do not like the current set of colors, you can change them by selecting the *Palette Colors* option. (This option is available only on EGA and VGA monitors.)

The Palette Colors dialog box displays the default set of 16 colors. Move the selection arrow to the color you want to change. The arrow can be moved by dragging with the mouse or by highlighting it and pressing the ↑ and ↓ keys. Select the *Change* option and then select a new color from the list of alternate colors.

Again, don't be afraid to experiment a little. The *Default* option returns the palette to its default colors.

## CHANGING THE VIDEO MODE

By default, there are 25 lines of text on your screen. If you have an EGA monitor, you can also display 35 or 43 lines. VGA allows 40 or 50 lines. Selecting the *Video Mode* option produces a simple dialog box. In it, select the radio button that represents the number of lines you wish to display on your screen and then select *OK*. (This option only works with EGA and VGA cards.)

# ADJUSTING KEYBOARD SENSITIVITY

All PC keyboards have *repeating keys*. This means that if you hold down a key, you will type the character over and over again. The *Keyboard Speed* option allows you to set the keyboard's *repeat rate* (the number of characters repeated per second) and the *repeat delay* (length of time a key must be held down before it starts repeating). People with heavy fingers might like to lengthen the repeat delay, while people with a lighter touch can shorten it. (This option will work on all 286-, 386-, and 486-based computers and on some 8088- and 8086-based computers.)

Selecting the *Keyboard Speed* option produces the dialog box shown in Figure 14.2. To adjust the repeat rate, highlight the *characters/second* label above the first "belt buckle," then slide the belt buckle itself by dragging with the mouse or using the ←

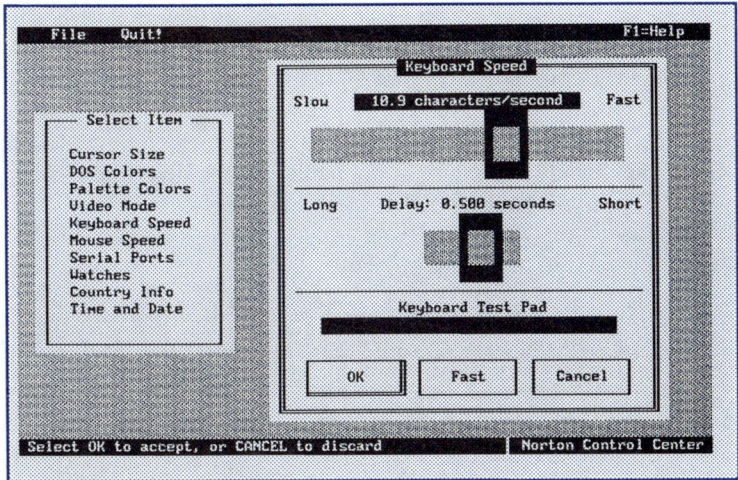

■ *Figure 14.2: The Keyboard Speed dialog box*

and → keys. The maximum setting is 30 characters per second; the minimum is 2.

Similarly, to adjust the repeat delay, highlight the *Delay:...* label above the second belt buckle. Slide the buckle to adjust the repeat delay.

You can test your setting by pressing and holding any key. The Keyboard Test Pad displays that setting's effect.

There is no default option for this function. Instead, the *Fast* option sets both the repeat rate and repeat delay to their maximum settings.

## ADJUSTING MOUSE SENSITIVITY

The feel of your mouse is a very personal thing. The *Mouse Speed* option allows you to adjust *mouse sensitivity* (the relationship between the movement of your mouse across the desktop and the movement of the mouse pointer on the screen).

Selecting the *Mouse Speed* option also produces a belt buckle. Slide the buckle to the right to make your mouse more sensitive. Slide it to the left to make it less sensitive.

You may want to keep in mind that:

- The effects of this option will be immediately noticeable, whereas the effects of others won't be noticeable until you quit NCC.

- The *Default* option sets mouse sensitivity back to the system default.

STEP
14

# SETTING SERIAL PORTS

This option allows you to set the configuration of your serial ports. While you will rarely need to do this, some serial devices, such as laser printers, may require it.

Selecting the *Serial Ports* option produces the Serial Ports dialog box. From it, select the port you wish to configure—available ports are listed at the top of the box—and the radio buttons representing the settings you want. For example, to set a serial port to "9600,N,8,1" select the radio buttons labeled *9600 Baud, No Parity, 8 Data Bits,* and *1 Stop Bit.*

# USING STOPWATCHES

You may occasionally find the need for a stopwatch. NCC provides four. Selecting the *Watches* option produces a dialog box with the four stopwatches. Select the radio button corresponding to the watch you want. Select the *Start* option to begin timing. Select the *Pause* option to stop a watch. Select the *Reset* option to set a watch to zero.

# CHANGING COUNTRY INFORMATION

The *Country Info* option allows you to change date, time, and currency formats. To use *Country Info,* you must first issue the command

```
nlsfunc \path\country.sys
```

where *path* is the directory in which the COUNTRY.SYS file is stored on your hard disk (usually \DOS). Then you can select the *Country Info* option, which displays a dialog box listing available country settings. Select the country that you want and the displayed time, date, and currency settings will change accordingly.

## SETTING SYSTEM DATE AND TIME

Computer clocks are noticeably inaccurate and, if you care about your system time and date, you may find yourself resetting them often. Selecting the *Time and Date* function brings up a dialog box showing the current system date and time. To make adjustments, highlight the month, day, or year in the box marked *Date,* or the hour, minute, or second in the box marked *Time.* You can change the settings incrementally with the + and − keys, or you can type your corrections.

## SAVING NCC CHANGES

After experimenting with NCC you may find that you would like to make a number of permanent changes to your system. It is not necessary to run NCC and reenter the changes you want each time you start your machine. Instead, you can save your changes in a file and call them automatically.

1.  Pull down the File menu and select *Save settings....*

2.  On the dialog box that appears, toggle on the configuration options you wish to save.

3.  In the File Name box, type a name for the configuration file (such as C:\NORTON\NCC.SET). You should preface the file name with a path.

4.  Select *OK.*

To load changes automatically, put the following command in your AUTOEXEC.BAT file:

```
ncc filename /set
```

*Filename* is the name (including the path) you entered for the configuration file in step 3 above.

# *Managing Directories*

A hard disk, even a relatively small one of 20 megabytes, can hold many hundreds of files. In order to bring some kind of coherent order to this space, you create subdirectories. However, as you create more and more of them, it can become more difficult to find your way around.

The Norton Change Directory (NCD) program is designed to make the task of managing your subdirectories easier. It not only allows you to move easily between subdirectories, it allows you to create, rename, and delete them as well. This step presents a short tutorial on NCD. It should take you about 30 minutes to complete.

## VIEWING AND
## PRINTING THE DIRECTORY TREE

Let's begin the tutorial by getting an overall picture of your hard disk's directory structure. Start NCD by entering

**ncd**

**STEP**

**15**

at the command prompt or by selecting the *Norton CD* option under the TOOLS topic in the Norton Utilities Shell. When the program starts, it will display all, or at least part, of your directory tree, as in Figure 15.1.

The root directory, C:\, appears at the top left of the tree as a backslash (\). Subdirectories of the root directory appear one column to the right of the root directory. Subdirectories of these directories appear one column further to the right, and so on. Making your way around your hard disk can be aided by referring to a printed copy of the directory tree. Print out a copy now.

1. Pull down the Directory menu and select the *Print tree...* option.

2. At the *Print the directory structure to:* prompt on the dialog box that appears, you specify the port to which your printer

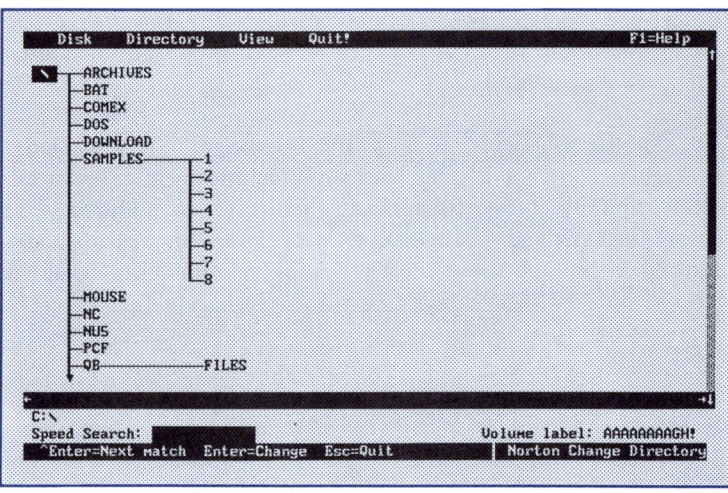

■ *Figure 15.1: A sample directory tree*

is attached. If it is attached to the first parallel port, and chances are it is, you do not need to change the default, PRN. The second parallel port is LPT2:, the first serial port is COM1:, the second is COM2:, and so on. If you are not certain which port your printer is attached to, do not change the default. If you are unable to print, check your printer manual or with your manufacturer's technical support department.

3.  In the Tree format box, select the *Tree, Graphic chars* option if your printer can print graphics. This option produces the nicest looking tree, connecting each of the subdirectories with an unbroken line. If your printer cannot print graphics, select the *Tree, Non-graphic chars* option. This option produces a tree with lines constructed with pluses and hyphens.

4.  Select the *Print* option to print the tree.

## NAVIGATING AMONG DIRECTORIES

Getting from one directory to the next from the DOS prompt is not difficult. The DOS CD (Change Directory) command will take you where you want to go. You may choose, however, to use NCD's tree to change directories as it allows you to "see" where you are going.

1.  Use the ↑ and ↓ keys to move the highlight bar to the \NORTON directory.

2.  Press Enter. This quits the program and returns you to DOS. (If you started NCD from the Shell, quit this as well.)

3.  Enter the DOS command

    `dir`

You will see the Norton Utilities files—the contents of the \NORTON directory.

4.  Restart NCD.

You can also move the highlight bar with the built-in Speed Search. Pressing a character key automatically moves the highlight to the first directory beginning with that character.

1.  Press \. This moves the highlight bar to the root directory.

2.  Press Backspace to erase the backslash from the Speed Search box at the bottom of the screen.

3.  Press **N**. This moves the highlight to the first directory beginning with N. To jump to the next one, press Ctrl-Enter.

## MAKING, DELETING, AND RENAMING DIRECTORIES

When it comes to directory maintenance, NCD provides the functions available to you in DOS (making and removing directories), and some functions that are not (renaming a directory and deleting a directory that is not empty).

1.  Move the highlight bar to the root directory.

2.  Make a new directory. Pull down the Directory menu and select the *Make* option.

3.  On the dialog box that appears, type

    `test18`

    and select *OK*.

4.  Press Enter to exit NCD and go to the new directory.

5.  Copy a few files into this directory. (Make sure to keep the originals. The files you copy into TEST18 will be deleted later in this exercise.)

6. Change to the root directory by entering the command

   **cd\**

   (You must do this to rename TEST18 as you cannot rename the current directory.)

7. Restart NCD and highlight the TEST18 directory.

8. Rename TEST18 to STEP18. Pull down the Directory
   menu and select the *Rename* option.

9. On the dialog box that appears, type

   **step18**

   and select *OK*. You will see the directory name change on
   the tree.

10. Pull down the Directory menu and select the *Delete* option.
    Now delete the STEP18 directory and all of the files in it.

11. In the warning dialog box, select the *Yes* option.

Unlike DOS, NCD allows you to delete directories containing
files. NCD does not, however, allow you to delete directories containing subdirectories. Attempting to do so will simply produce an
error message.

This brings you to the end of the tutorial. To quit the program,
change to a directory of your choice by pressing enter. Alternatively, you can quit by selecting *Quit!* from the menu bar.

# Configuration Information

The Norton Utilities package provides a powerful diagnostic tool in the SYSINFO program, which tells you nearly everything you ever wanted to know about the configuration of your computer, both inside and out. This step presents a brief tutorial that takes you through some of the more accessible screens. The remaining screens are summarized for your reference.

## RUNNING SYSINFO

Start the program by entering

```
sysinfo
```

from the DOS command line, or

```
si
```

if you renamed this program during installation. Alternatively, you can select the *System Info* option under the TOOLS topic in the Norton Utilities Shell.

When the program starts, you will see the System Summary screen shown in Figure 16.1.

**System summary**

This screen is effectively SYSINFO's main screen as it always comes up when you start the program. It details the basic configuration of your computer. For example, the computer from which this image was taken is an 80386 machine running at 25 megahertz with VGA graphics. It has a 78 megabyte hard disk with two high-density floppy drives.

At the bottom of this screen, and on the bottom of each of the sixteen other information screens, are the four options listed below:

- *Next:* Displays the next information screen in the sequence. Screens are ordered as the pull-down menus are on the

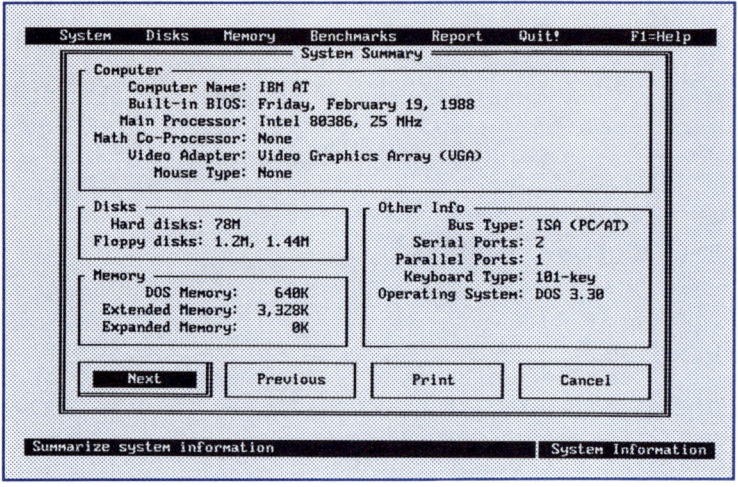

• *Figure 16.1: The System Summary screen*

menu bar (the first screen comes from the first option on the System menu, the last from the last option on the Report menu).

■ *Previous:* Displays the previous information screen in the sequence described above.

■ *Print:* Prints (to a printer or to a file) the information on a given screen.

■ *Cancel:* Closes the current screen and returns you to the menu bar.

Let's move on from System Summary to some different screens. Pull down the Benchmarks menu and select the *CPU speed...* option. This brings up the screen shown in Figure 16.2.

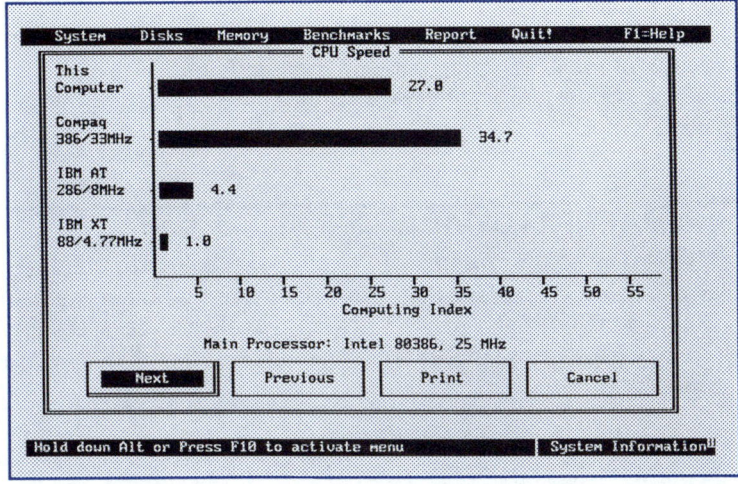

■ *Figure 16.2: The CPU Benchmark*

*CPU*
*speed*

The bar graph on this screen shows the speed of your main processor, the IBM AT, and the Compaq 386/33 relative to that of the IBM XT. As you can see, the AT is 4.4 times faster than the XT, the Compaq is almost 35 times faster than the XT, while the machine from which this image was taken is 27 times faster.

*Hard disk*
*speed*

Pull down the Benchmarks menu and select the *Hard disk speed...* option. This option produces a screen similar to that shown on the previous page, though this time the graph represents relative speeds of hard disks. The most useful information on this screen may well be the Average Seek Time (also called Average Access Time) figure near the bottom. This is a measure of the amount of time it takes for the read/write heads on your hard disk to find some given data. It is the number used in many stores and magazines to compare hard disk speeds.

*Memory-*
*resident*
*programs*

Finally, pull down the Memory menu and select the *TSR programs...* option. This produces a screen displaying some fairly obscure information, though in the Owner column you will see a list of the memory-resident programs currently loaded in your computer's memory.

## REMAINING SCREENS

This brings you to the end of the tutorial. The remaining thirteen screens are summarized below by option name within menu name. Keep in mind that every SYSINFO screen can be accessed in the same way: just pull down a menu and select the appropriate option.

## System Menu Screens

- *Video summary:* Gives information about your video card and monitor (the kind of graphics standard installed, the current video mode, the number of lines that can be displayed on screen, etc.)

- *Hardware interrupts:* Lists current hardware interrupts. A hardware interrupt is the means by which a device, such as a floppy disk or a parallel port, lets the CPU know that there is an operation to carry out.

- *Software interrupts:* Lists current software interrupts. Performs the same function as a hardware interrupt, but for software instead.

- *Network Information:* Displays information about the current user and the kind of network the user is working on.

- *CMOS status:* Displays current settings stored in CMOS, such as the number and type of drives installed on your machine. The CMOS is the means by which 286-, 386-, and 486-class machines remember what is installed on the system (the kind of floppy disks, amount of memory, the type and size of hard disk, etc.), as well and the date and time.

## The Disks Menu

- *Disk Summary:* Provides information on all drives installed on your computer—the drive letters assigned to them, their size, their current default directory.

- *disk Characteristics:* Gives the logical and physical characteristics on any specific drive on your computer—the size of sectors and clusters, the number of sectors occupied by data, etc.

- *Partition Tables:* Gives the location and contents of your partition table. Roughly speaking, the partition table lists the logical segments into which your hard disk is divided, whether you have multiple logical drives (C:, D:, E:), and so on.

## The Memory Menu

- *memory Usage summary:* Describes the kind and amount of memory installed in your computer (conventional, extended, or expanded memory), how much of it is used, and how much is free.

- *memory Block list:* Details your 640K of conventional memory, which programs are loaded, their locations in memory, and more.

- *Device drivers:* Lists the device drivers currently loaded on your system. Device drivers are required to run certain peripherals (such as mice and scanners) and programs and applications. These are most frequently loaded in your CONFIG.SYS file with the DEVICE= statement.

## The Benchmarks Menu

- *Overall Performance Index:* Combines the functions of the CPU and hard disk benchmarks discussed above in such a way as to compare the overall speed of your machine to Compaq and IBM computers.

- *Network performance speed:* Tests the hard disk of your network server, measuring its "throughput" in kilobytes per second.

# The Report Menu

- *view AUTOEXEC.BAT:* Allows you to view the contents of your AUTOEXEC.BAT file.

- *view CONFIG.SYS:* Allows you to view the contents of your CONFIG.SYS file.

# *Enhancing Batch Files*

*Batch files* are executable files that run a series of DOS commands. To execute all the commands contained in a batch file, you simply type its file name. For example, given an appropriate batch file, you could execute—in one action—the commands to clear the screen, to change a directory, and to run the program you want.

You create and edit batch files with a word processor. You must place each command on its own line and save the file in ASCII format. If you need more information on how to create, edit, or execute batch files, refer to your DOS manual.

This step introduces you to the BE (Batch Enhancer) program, which provides a number of features you can use to beef up your batch files: sound, boxes, windows, timed delays, color, and cursor control. The BE program is different from most of the other Norton Utilities in that it does not have an interactive interface—no dialog boxes, pull down menus, or radio buttons. Its commands are all executed from within batch files.

This step, then, differs from other steps accordingly. Here, instead of a tutorial, you will find a section devoted to each BE command. Each section will provide syntax with explanations and an example. Take some time to read through the step and see what you might find useful or what piques your interest. Trying them all should take you about 45 minutes.

## DECIPHERING SYNTAX

Syntax listings in this step use a few conventions you should be aware of. The command you type in at the DOS prompt is displayed directly below the "Syntax" heading. Following this, optional elements such as command line switches appear in parentheses. Arguments, the places where you supply file names or integers, appear in italics. Mutually exclusive options are separated by a vertical bar (This|That). Toward the end of each section, an example is given to illustrate the command's practical use. (Please note: BE commands should be typed as one line, but examples are sometimes displayed on two lines to accommodate the margins of this book.)

## USER-DEFINED MENUS

One of the more useful BE commands is ASK, which allows you to put user-defined menus in your batch files. This command requires knowledge of DOS batch file programming. Because this is an advanced subject, it cannot be treated extensively in a book of this length; however, an example will be provided.

## Syntax

```
BE ASK "prompt", (keys) (default=key)
(timeout=secs) (color)
```

**"prompt"** is the text you wish to display. It is a good idea to list available menu choices here. **"prompt"** must be enclosed in quotes.

**keys** displays a list of those keys that are valid responses to prompt (e.g., **abcd**). The user must press one of these keys in response to your menu. Pressing any other key produces an error beep.

**default=***key* specifies the default key. That is, if the user waits too long without making a choice (see **timeout** below), the default key is automatically selected.

**timeout=***secs* specifies the amount of time the ASK command will wait before automatically selecting the default key (see **default** above). If this option is not specified, ASK will wait indefinitely.

**color** specifies the color of the box. Valid colors are black, blue, green, cyan, red, magenta, yellow, white, gray, bright blue, bright green, bright cyan, bright red, bright magenta, bright yellow, and bright white.

## Example

To gain a more practical understanding of ASK, let's create a short batch file that allows the user to format a floppy in drive A or drive B using the SFORMAT program. When this batch file is executed, the user need only press **A** to format the floppy in drive A or **B** to format the floppy in drive B. If ten seconds expire before a key is pressed, ASK selects **A** by default.

This batch file effectively has two parts. The first line is a concrete example of the general ASK syntax you saw above. The second section (everything that follows the first line) is DOS batch command language. For now, don't worry if you don't understand this second part; it will be explained below.

```
be ask "Format A or B", ab default=a timeout=10
    if errorlevel 2 goto :driveb
    if errorlevel 1 goto :drivea
:driveb
    sformat b:
    goto :end
:drivea
    sformat a:
    goto :end
:end
```

The DOS batch file programming language is somewhat obscure at first, but once it is broken down into its components, you'll find it quite straightforward. The first two lines, called IF ERROR-LEVEL commands, don't actually have anything to do with errors. They are, rather, if-then statements. For example,

**if errorlevel 2 goto :driveb**

means "if you press the second key in the key list (**B**) the program will skip to the label **:driveb** and follow the commands there (**sformat b:** and then **goto :end** to skip to the end of the file)." Similarly,

**if errorlevel 1 goto :drivea**

means "if you press the first key in the key list (**A**), the program will skip to the label **:drivea** and follow the commands there (**sformat a:**, etc.)."

Keep in mind the following points:

■ There should be one IF ERRORLEVEL statement for each key that you list as a valid response.

- The IF ERRORLEVEL statements must themselves be listed in descending order (**if errorlevel 3** before **if errorlevel 2** before **if errorlevel 1**).

Labels (**:drivea** and **:driveb** in the example above) are used to demarcate different groups of commands within a batch file. If you choose one option, the batch file will perform one set of commands marked by a certain label (the commands immediately following the label and preceding the next label). If you choose another option, the batch file will perform a second, separate set of commands. Notice that, in the example, each set of commands ends with a command to go to the end of the batch file. Inserting such commands is a good practice as it ensures the execution of only one group of commands at a time. *Labels*

## USING SOUND (BEEP)

Occasionally you will find it necessary to attract a user's attention—at the end of a lengthy operation, for example. The BEEP command allows you to play tones of specified duration and pitch.

## Syntax

```
BE BEEP (/D#) (/F#) (/R#) (/W#)
```

**/D#** specifies the duration of the tone in eighteenths of a second (**/D9** plays a tone for half a second, **/D18** for one second, etc.).

**/F#** specifies the frequency of a tone in hertz. **/F440** plays middle C.

**/R#** specifies the number of times a tone is repeated.

/W# specifies the interval between tones in eighteenths of a second.

## Example

The following command plays three middle Cs lasting half a second each with one second in between:

```
BE BEEP /D9 /F440 /R3 /W18
```

## Alternate Syntax

```
BE BEEP filename (/E)
```

The BEEP command has an alternate syntax if you wish to save a group of notes for repeated use. Instead of listing BEEP commands on a line in your batch file, you can store them in a separate tone file.

*filename* is the name of your tone file. The tone file must be in ASCII format. Tones are specified in this file by using the switches listed above, just as they are on the command line.

/E allows you to echo comments in the tone file to the screen. Comments must be enclosed in quotation marks and be separated from the tone command switches by a semicolon.

## Example

The following tone file will play two half-second middle Cs and two half-second Cs one octave above middle C, with comments appearing on your screen at the appropriate time.

```
/D9 /F440 /R2 /W9;"Two Middle Cs"
/D9 /F880 /R2 /W9;"Two Cs above that"
```

## DRAWING BOXES

The BOX command allows you to draw boxes on your screen
with great ease. This can spiff up the look of your batch files.

## Syntax

**BE BOX** *RowTLC ColTLC RowBRC ColBRC*
(Single|Double) (*color*)

*RowTLC* and *ColTLC* are the screen coordinates of the top left
corner of the box. *RowTLC* is the row in which this corner sits,
and *ColTLC* is the column. The top row of your screen is row 0,
the bottom row is usually 24, though if you are using a high-
resolution EGA or VGA mode the value may be larger. The leftmost column is 0, the rightmost is 79.

*RowBRC* and *ColBRC* are the screen coordinates of the bottom
right corner of the box. The values you can use to specify these
coordinates are given in the paragraph above.

**Single|Double** specifies whether the box is drawn with single or
double lines.

*color* specifies the color of the box. Valid colors are the same as
those for the ASK command.

## Example

To draw a single-line green box roughly in the center of your screen, enter the following command:

```
BE BOX 7 20 17 60 single green
```

## PAUSING

Occasionally you will find it useful to pause your batch files for a short period of time. The DELAY command pauses a batch file for a specified amount of time.

## Syntax

```
BE DELAY #
```

# specifies the length of the delay in eighteenths of a second.

## Example

This command causes the batch file to pause for five seconds:

```
BE DELAY 90
```

## PRINTING REPEATING CHARACTERS

The BE commands give you a good amount of control over the way things appear on your screen. The PRINTCHAR command is a limited, but occasionally useful, tool that allows you to write a character on the screen a specified number of times.

## Syntax

```
BE PRINTCHAR Char # (color)
```

***Char*** is the character to be written on screen. Any character on the keyboard can be used.

# is the number of times you want to write ***Char***.

***color*** specifies the color in which the character(s) should be written. Valid colors are the same as those for the ASK command.

## Example

To write a line of 25 bright red exclamation points, enter the following command:

```
BE PRINTCHAR ! 25 bright red
```

# POSITIONING THE CURSOR

Boxes and windows aren't much use unless you have a way of putting something in them, and repeating characters really require that you be able to position them as you please. The ROWCOL command allows you to jump the cursor to any location on the screen and, optionally, write text there. This allows you to put text anywhere within a box or window and position repeating text as well.

## Syntax

```
BE ROWCOL row col ("text") (color)
```

*row* is the row on the screen where you wish to position the cursor. The top row of the screen is 0 and the bottom is usually 24, though if you are using a high-resolution EGA or VGA mode, this number might be larger.

*col* is the column on the screen where you wish to position the cursor. The leftmost column is 0, the rightmost, 79.

**"text"** is the text you wish to write at the new cursor position. This text must be enclosed in quotation marks.

*color* is the color of **"text"**. Valid colors are the same as those for the ASK command.

## Example

To write the text *Step 17* in the sample box we created previously, place the following commands in a batch file:

```
BE BOX 7 20 17 60 single green
BE ROWCOL 12 36 "Step 17" bright white
```

## SETTING SCREEN ATTRIBUTES

Through the SA (Screen Attributes) command, the BE program gives your batch files control over screen colors: the color of the text, the background, and the screen border. Although this command duplicates one of the functions of the Norton Control Center (NCC) program, it remains in the current version of the Norton Utilities because SA was an independent program in previous versions.

For the SA command to work successfully, the ANSI.SYS driver must be loaded on your system. This can be accomplished by adding the following line to your CONFIG.SYS file and rebooting your computer:

```
device=\path\ansi.sys
```

*path* is the directory in which ANSI.SYS is located.

## Syntax

```
BE SA (intensity) (textcolor) (ON background)
(/N) (/CLS)
```

*intensity* specifies the intensity of your text. This option can be set to *Bright,* which causes text to appear more brightly than is usual, or *Blinking,* which causes text to blink.

*textcolor* specifies the color of the text. Valid colors are black, blue, green, cyan, red, magenta, yellow, and white.

*background* specifies the color of the screen background. Valid colors for this option are the same as for *textcolor.*

**/N** leaves the border color unchanged. That is, normally the border color is automatically set to the background color. Use this switch to change background color but not the border color.

**/CLS** clears the screen after you change screen colors.

## Example

This command is fairly straightforward. To set the screen colors to bright green text on a black background, as in the original IBM

PC, enter the following in a batch file:

**BE SA bright green on black**

## Syntax

**BE SA *default* (/N) (/CLS)**

The SA command also gives you a quick way to reset the screen to its original colors. This second command syntax manipulates the default display colors (white text on a black background).

*default* specifies how to treat the default colors. This option may be set to *Normal* (white text on a black background), *Reverse* (black text on a white background), or *Underline* (underlined white text on a black background).

/**N** is the same as for the above SA syntax.

/**CLS** is the same as for the above SA syntax.

## Example

If you've been experimenting with different color combinations and wish to reset your screen colors, enter the following:

**BE SA normal**

## DRAWING WINDOWS

The WINDOW command, like the BOX command, makes for a good-looking screen. A window is a close cousin of a box, differing slightly in appearance and presentation.

# Syntax

```
BE WINDOW RowTLC ColTLC RowBRC ColBRC
(explode) (shadow) (color)
```

*RowTLC* and *ColTLC* are the screen coordinates of the top left corner of the window. *RowTLC* is the row in which this corner sits, and *ColTLC* is the column. The top row of your screen is row 0, the bottom row is usually 24, though if you are using a high-resolution EGA or VGA mode it may be larger. The leftmost column is 0, the right is 79.

*RowBRC* and *ColBRC* are the screen coordinates of the bottom right corner of the window. The values you use to specify these coordinates are given in the paragraph above.

**explode** causes the window to "explode" or expand outward from its center to its final position when it is drawn.

**shadow** draws a shadow along the right and bottom edges of the window, thus giving the window a three-dimensional look on color displays. The shadow does not obscure text underneath it.

*color* specifies the color of the window. Valid colors are listed as for the ASK command.

# Example

Enter the following command to draw a green window at the same location used in the BOX example above. In addition, the window will "explode" and have a 3D appearance.

```
BE WINDOW 7 20 17 60 explode shadow green
```

# *Optimizing*
# *Your Hard Disk I*

■ ■ ■ ■ ■ ■ ■ ■ ■ ■ ■

This step discusses the CALIBRAT program. It is the first of two steps on the subject of optimizing the performance of your hard disk and the first of three steps on optimizing your computer's overall speed.

The CALIBRAT program optimizes the performance of your hard disk in two different ways: it checks and optionally changes your *hard disk interleave,* and it tests the integrity of every single byte on the disk to make certain data can be written and read accurately. This step shows you how to perform both of these tests. However, before we actually run the program, let's discuss further what it means to optimize your interleave and test disk integrity.

## OPTIMIZING INTERLEAVE

For "bookkeeping" purposes, each sector on your hard disk is numbered. When consecutively numbered sectors are placed next to one another, the disk is said to have a 1:1 (one to one) interleave; when they are placed every other sector, the disk has a

2:1 interleave; when they are located every third sector, the disk has a 3:1 interleave, and so on. To optimize your interleave means to choose the ratio that makes most efficient use of your hard disk.

Because hard disks spin at a constant rate, different interleave settings will cause data to be written to or read from your hard disk at different rates. Some interleave settings will require more revolutions of the disk (and therefore more time) to read or write the same data. CALIBRAT can change the interleave on your hard disk to an optimal setting: the one that requires the fewest revolutions of the disk, and therefore the least amount of time, to read and write data. If the interleave is not optimally set, changing it can speed up your system considerably.

**Low-level formats**

Changing interleaves is accomplished by performing a *low-level format* on your hard disk. Low-level formats are usually done on hard disks by the manufacturer or dealer and are different from the kind of formats you are used to performing. Thus you may never have heard of low-level formats, much less have had to perform one. Low-level formats set such things as your hard disk interleave, the size of clusters, and so on; and normally they destroy any data on the disk (one of the reasons no DOS program is provided for this purpose). However, CALIBRAT's low-level format adjusts your hard disk interleave *without destroying any data.*

## PATTERN TESTING

CALIBRAT tests disk integrity by running a *pattern test*. In other words, CALIBRAT writes patterns of 0s and 1s to each sector on the disk and then reads them. If any errors are found in the reading, the cluster is marked as bad and is taken out of use by DOS. If there is any data on the cluster, it is moved to a healthy area of the disk. The clusters that remain after pattern testing are, therefore, suitable for use. Pattern testing does no damage to data already on your disk.

# PREPARING TO RUN CALIBRAT

Before you run CALIBRAT, please read through the following precautionary points:

1.  *Back up your hard disk first* just in case something goes wrong (such as a power outage). There is a *remote* chance that data will be lost.

2.  Do *not* run CALIBRAT on any of the following kinds of drives, as you can severely damage them:

    ■   Hard disks with SCSI or IDE controllers. If you don't know if your hard disk is one of these types, consult your documentation, dealer, or technical support.

    ■   Hard disk controllers that use *sector translation;* that is, controllers that fool DOS into thinking that the number of sectors on each disk track is different from what it actually is. Again, if you are uncertain about your hard disk, consult your documentation, dealer, or technical support.

    ■   Hard disk controllers that have built-in disk caches.

You should run CALIBRAT at the end of the day or overnight. The low-level format, which is actually done simultaneously with pattern testing, can take many hours.

# RUNNING CALIBRAT

To run CALIBRAT, do the following:

1.  Start the program by entering

    `calibrat`

    at the command line or by selecting the *Calibrate* option under the SPEED topic in the Norton Utilities Shell.

2. On the information dialog box that appears, select the *Continue* option when you are finished reading.

3. From the drive list, select the drive to optimize (*C:*).

4. On the caution dialog box that reminds you to back up your data, select the *Continue* option when you are finished reading.

5. On the information dialog box listing the tests that will be performed, select *Continue* when you are finished reading. This causes CALIBRAT to begin testing.

## System Integrity Testing

In addition to the optimization functions discussed at the beginning of this step, CALIBRAT runs a set of tests on your hard disk and related system components. The first test, called System Integrity Testing, checks to make sure that various components and functions integral to the working of your hard disk do, in fact, work properly. This test checks your computer's RAM, the RAM on your hard disk controller, the controller itself, and more. The System Integrity Testing screen is shown in Figure 18.1.

If CALIBRAT finds any errors here, it cannot repair them; you will need to contact your dealer or manufacturer for asssistance.

## Seek Tests

*Relative hard disk speed*

When the System Integrity Tests are complete, CALIBRAT goes right into the second set of tests, called Seek Tests. The Seek Tests are a measure of the speed of your hard disk. The most useful of these tests is the Average Seek Test, also called Average Access Time. It measures the average amount of time it takes to find a file on your hard disk. This is the figure used in the industry to

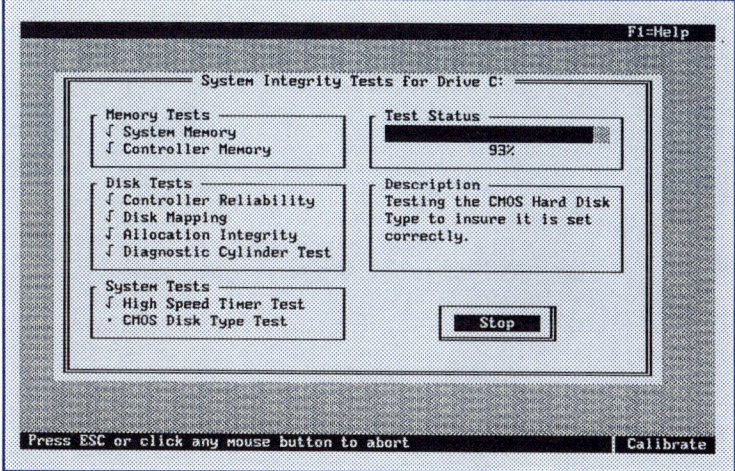

■ *Figure 18.1: The System Integrity Testing screen*

compare relative hard disk speeds (it is the figure most often cited by hard disk manufacturers and sellers). The Seek Tests screen is shown in Figure 18.2.

# Data Encoding Tests

Select the *Continue* option when you are finished examining the results of the Seek Tests. This starts the Data Encoding Tests, which determine the speed at which your hard disk spins (3600 rpm), the kind of hard disk controller you have, and its method of writing data on the hard disk. This information can be useful if you are replacing your hard disk controller (as controller types are distinguished by the way they encode data on the hard disk) or for diagnostic purposes. The Data Encoding Tests screen is shown in Figure 18.3.

*Hard disk controller*

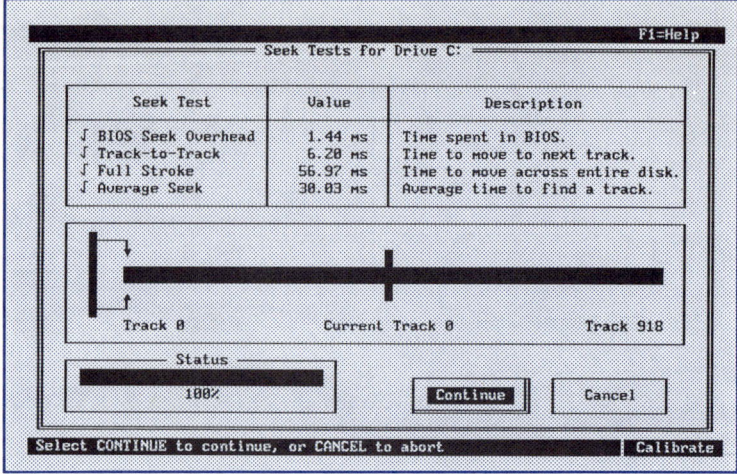

- *Figure 18.2: The Seek Tests screen*

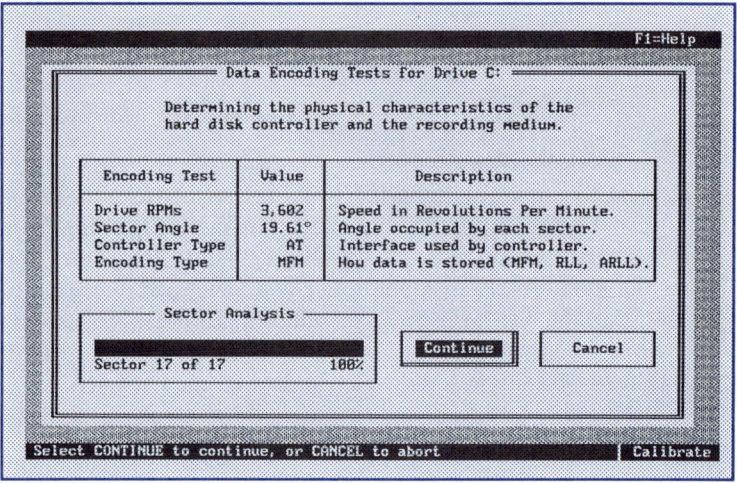

- *Figure 18.3: The Data Encoding Tests screen*

# Interleave Testing

Select the *Continue* option when you are finished reading the Data Encoding Tests screen. This starts Interleave Testing. CALIBRAT determines your current hard disk interleave and checks other interleave settings to see which will allow your computer to read and write data the fastest. Specifically, it checks interleaves 1:1 through 8:1 and graphs them as a function of the number of revolutions required to read one track. (Data on a disk is laid out in concentric circles called tracks. One track is simply one circle of data, often made up of 17 sectors.) The results of a test on my machine are shown in Figure 18.4.

As you can see from Figure 18.4, the current setting of the hard disk is marked *Current* and the optimal setting is marked *Optimal*.

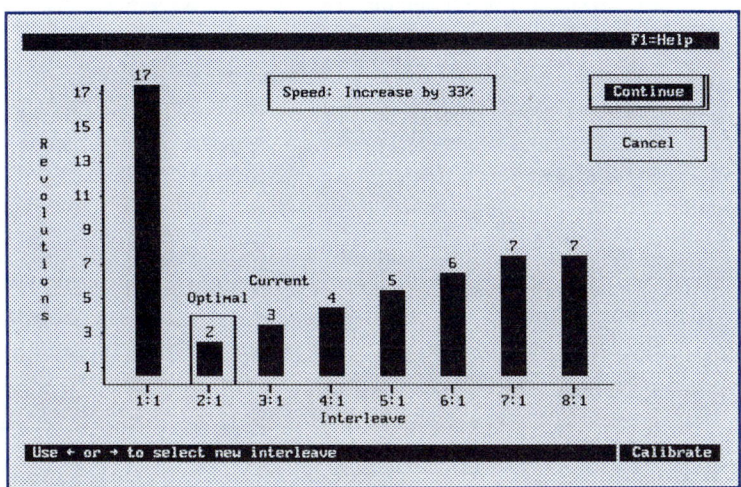

- *Figure 18.4: Interleave Testing results*

If your hard disk's current setting is not its optimal one, you should change it. To do this:

1.  Use the ← and → keys to move the highlight box (the rectangular box surrounding the 2:1 bar in Figure 18.4) to the *Optimal* setting. The increase in speed, if any, will appear in the speed box at the top of the screen. CALIBRAT will reformat your hard disk to the interleave you specify with the highlight box.

2.  Select the *Continue* option.

3.  On the dialog box that appears, select the radio button representing the level of pattern testing you want. Keep in mind this will take many hours to complete. If you do not want to run pattern testing, you may select the *No pattern testing* option. Selecting the *Rigorous* option will find errors that have not yet surfaced. If you have not previously run CALIBRAT, you should select this option. (On subsequent uses of the program, you may select one of the less rigorous pattern tests.)

4.  When you have selected the level of pattern testing, select the *OK* option to start resetting the interleave and pattern testing.

5.  When it is finished, the program provides a report of its findings and its work. Select the *Print* option to print the report or the *Save as...* option to save it as a text file. Select the *Done* option, whether or not you have printed the report, to quit the program.

# Optimizing
# Your Hard Disk II

When you write a file to your disk, the first part of the file is placed in the first empty space on your disk. (Disk space is divided into clusters, or units of 2,048 bytes. A byte is the amount of space occupied by one character.) The next part of the file is placed in the next available space, and so on, filling the disk from front to back. As a result, when files are copied onto an empty hard disk, each file's parts (or clusters) sit together in one area of the disk.

On a disk that has seen much use, however, files can be scattered over different areas of a disk. This happens because of the way in which vacated space is filled. When a 20 kilobyte (20K) file is deleted, it opens up a 20K space on your disk. If a 25K file is then copied onto the disk, the first 20K of the new file is put into the vacated space while the remaining part of the file must be placed elsewhere. This fragmenting of files is a normal artifact of DOS bookkeeping and you probably won't notice it—until your hard disk slows down. When files become scattered, the read/write heads on your hard disk (the recording heads that read and write data to and from your disk) have to travel all over the disk just to find one file. The further they have to travel and the more they have to whip back and forth, the longer it takes. If many of your files are fragmented, you may notice that it takes longer to read files than it did when your hard disk was new.

The SPEEDISK program optimizes your hard disk performance by unfragmenting the files on your disk—putting all parts of each file together—thereby reversing the retarding effect of file fragmentation.

This step contains a tutorial in which you will unfragment your hard disk. Since the functions of the DS (Directory Sort) program from version 4.5 are included in SPEEDISK, you will also sort the directories on your hard disk. The process of unfragmenting files can take some time, depending on how large your hard disk is and how many files you have on it, so you should plan on this step taking you up to 45 minutes.

## UNFRAGMENTING FILES ON YOUR HARD DISK

If you are going to work through this tutorial, it would be prudent to be absolutely safe and *back up your hard disk* before you begin. It is *very unlikely* that you will lose any data, but if a power failure does occur while SPEEDISK is optimizing your disk, you may lose some files.

## STARTING SPEEDISK

To begin the tutorial and the process of optimizing your disk, do the following:

1. Start the SPEEDISK program by entering

   `speedisk`

at the command line or selecting the *Speed Disk* option under the SPEED topic in the Norton Utilities shell. (Type **SD** if you renamed the program during installation.)

2. On the list that appears, select your hard disk (*C:*) and select *OK*.

3. SPEEDISK reports on the extent of file fragmentation and recommends a method of optimization, as in Figure 19.1.

SPEEDISK can optimize your disk in four different ways:

▪ *Full Optimization:* This unfragments all files and moves all files and directories to the front of the disk. This option returns your disk to the state it was in when programs were first loaded onto it. It is the most ambitious and effective method of optimization and, as such, it takes the longest.

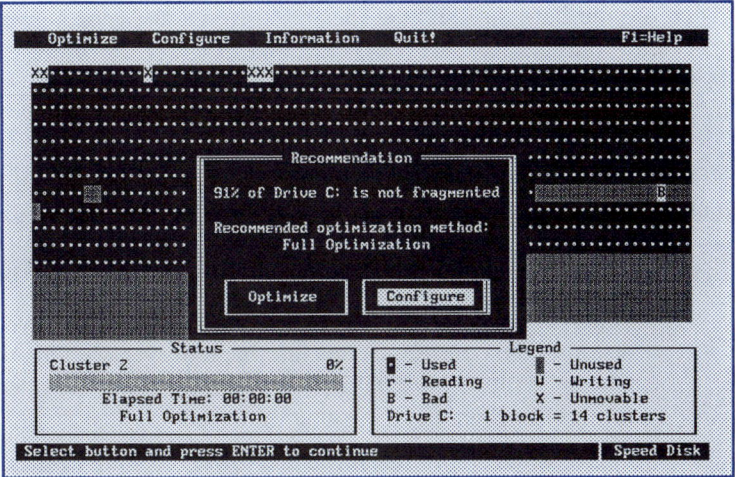

▪ *Figure 19.1: The Fragmentation Recommendation screen*

■ *Unfragment Files Only:* This simply unfragments your files without moving them forward on the disk. This method is faster than *Full Optimization* but not as thorough, as empty spaces will be left between files. Your disk is, therefore, likely to become fragmented again more quickly than if you use *Full Optimization*.

■ *Unfragment Free Space:* This method does not actually unfragment files. It simply moves data forward to the beginning of the disk and "plugs holes." Though faster than either of the previous options, it is not as effective.

■ *Directory Optimization:* This method is the least effective of all, moving no files but only directories forward to the beginning of the disk.

In addition to displaying SPEEDISK's recommendation, the Fragmentation Recommendation screen displays a pictoral representation of your hard disk and the files on it. Notice the gaps between occupied clusters.

## UNFRAGMENTING FILES

Once you have finished reading SPEEDISK's report, you can go ahead and optimize your hard disk. To do so, follow these steps:

1. Select the *Configure* option. If you want to accept SPEEDISK's recommendation, you can select the *Optimize* option at this point and move right into unfragmenting your disk. For the purposes of this tutorial, however, we will take the long way around so that you will see how to select the optimization method manually.

2. Pull down the Optimize menu and select the *Optimization Method...* option. This brings up the Select Optimization Method dialog box shown in Figure 19.2.

3.  Select the *Full Optimization* radio button for the most thorough optimization of your disk.

4.  Select the *OK* option.

5.  The Optimize menu is still pulled down. Select the *Begin optimization* option to unfragment your disk.

6.  After SPEEDISK is done, and this may take a while, select *OK* to acknowledge completion.

7.  Select the *Configure* option on the menu that appears to remain in the program.

The first half of the tutorial is finished and you have optimized your disk. Depending on how badly your files were fragmented, you may notice that things are running a bit faster now.

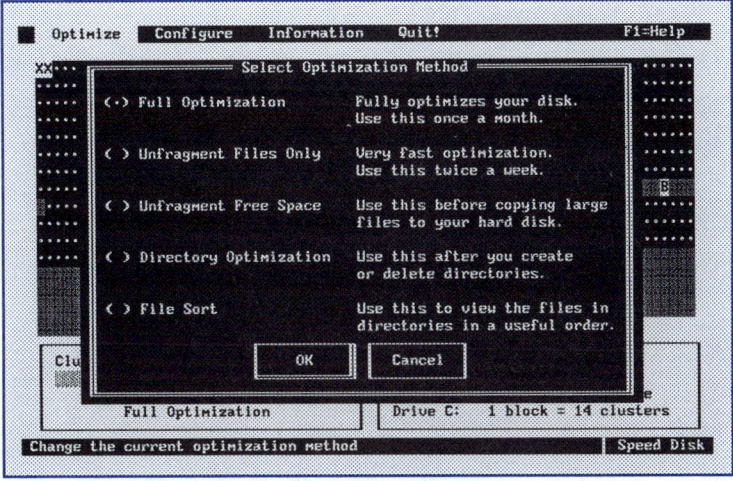

■ *Figure 19.2: The Select Optimization Method*

You will also notice on the map that all of the gaps between occupied clusters have been filled and that all of your data has been moved to the front of the disk.

## SORTING FILES IN THEIR DIRECTORIES

If you work with computers regularly, you have probably noticed that the DOS DIR command lists files in no particular order. (Actually, the files are listed in the order they were added to the directory.) This is not terribly conducive to finding a file in the DIR listing, especially if there are a large number of files. SPEEDISK can remedy the situation by sorting the files for you in some coherent order.

In the second half of this tutorial you will sort the directories on your hard disk by file name. If you followed the ten steps above, the *Configure* menu should still be pulled down. Select the *File sort...* option.

On the dialog box that appears, you will see the criteria by which you can sort your directory listings. These are explained in Table 19.1 below.

| Criterion | Effect |
|---|---|
| Unsorted | None (Files listed in order added) |
| Name | Sort by file name |
| Extension | Sort by file extension |
| Date & Time | Sort by file date |
| Size | Sort by file size |

*Table 19.1: File sort criteria*

| Criterion | Effect |
|-----------|--------|
| Ascending | Sort files A–Z, 1–9, etc. |
| Descending | Sort files Z–A, 9–1, etc. |

*Table 19.1: File sort criteria (continued)*

To proceed with the sort, follow these steps:

1. Select the *Name* and *Ascending* radio buttons; then select the *OK* option.

2. Pull down the Optimize menu and select the *Optimization Method...* option as you did in step 2 of the previous exercise.

3. Select the *File Sort* radio button and the *OK* option.

4. Select the *Begin optimization* option on the Optimize menu to sort your directory listings. It will not take long.

5. Select *OK* to acknowledge completion of the sort.

6. Select the *Exit to DOS* option.

7. To see the results of your work, enter the DOS command

   ```
   DIR
   ```

Sorting files in this way, though effective enough, may seem a bit cumbersome to users familiar with the DS program from version 4.5. Fortunately, there is a shortcut available. To sort your directories as we sorted them in the above exercise, enter the following at the command line:

```
speedisk c: /sn
```

This means "run SPEEDISK on drive C and sort by file name." The other sort criteria are also available, as shown in Table 19.2.

| Criteria | Syntax |
|---|---|
| Extension | speedisk c: /se |
| Date and Time | speedisk c: /sd |
| Size | speedisk c: /ss |

*Table 19.2: Command line sorting shortcuts*

By default, these commands sort in ascending order. To sort in descending order, add a hyphen to the end of the command as follows:

```
speedisk c: /sn-
```

# *Disk Caching*

One of the most effective ways to improve the performance of your computer is to use a disk cache. A cache is simply a section of memory into which data is placed after it is read from your disk. When this data is needed again, it can be taken directly from the memory cache rather than from the disk again. Since reading data from memory can be up to 200 times faster than reading data from a floppy and up to 65 times faster than reading from a hard disk, your system will work much more quickly.

The Norton Utilities provides two disk caching programs, NCACHE-F (Fast Cache) and NCACHE-S (Small Cache). The one you should use depends on the configuration of the computer you use.

You should use the Small Cache, NCACHE-S, if your computer has a limited amount of memory. In this context, that means a machine with no more than 640K of memory or a machine with 1Mb of memory that you keep loaded to the gills with memory-resident (TSR) programs. In short, NCACHE-S should be used on

*Small Cache*

XT computers or machines lacking any extended or expanded memory.

*Fast Cache*    The Fast Cache, NCACHE-F, should be used on machines that do not suffer such memory limitations. These are usually 80286-, 80386-, or 80486-based computers that have more than 1Mb of memory.

This step presents a short exercise on the use of the Norton caches. You will learn how to load, configure and reconfigure them. You should be able to work through this step in about 15 minutes.

## LOADING A CACHE

The cache programs, unlike most other Norton programs, do not have an interactive interface—no dialog boxes, pull-down menus, toggle options, or radio buttons. Instead, all configuration options are specified when the programs are run and the caches are loaded. The caches themselves are memory-resident (TSR) programs and therefore need be loaded only once per session.

Running the programs and loading the caches can be done in two different ways: through the AUTOEXEC.BAT file or through the CONFIG.SYS file. However, loading through AUTOEXEC.BAT is manifestly superior, as caches loaded through the CONFIG.SYS cannot be reconfigured without editing the CONFIG.SYS file and rebooting your machine. Loading a cache through your CONFIG.SYS will not, therefore, be done in this exercise.

Running one of the cache programs is as simple as adding a line like the following to your AUTOEXEC.BAT file:

```
c:\norton\ncache-f /options
```

At the end of this line, *options* represents the different possible configuration options. These are listed below:

- /DOS=*bytes*:  The cache uses conventional memory (memory that is part of the main 640K of memory) and is *bytes* kilobytes large.

- /EXT=*bytes*:  The cache uses extended memory (memory above the first megabyte of memory) and is *bytes* kilobytes large. You can load part of the cache into extended memory and part into conventional DOS memory by combining this option with the option above.

- /EXP=*bytes*:  The cache uses expanded memory (memory above the first megabyte configured by a special driver and/or memory board to the Lotus-Intel-Microsoft specification) and is *bytes* kilobytes large. You can load part of the cache into expanded memory and part into conventional DOS memory by combining this option with the /DOS option above.

You should use as much memory as you can spare when making the cache. The larger the cache, the more data it can store, and the faster your machine can work. The machine on which this book was written, for example, has about three megabytes of extended memory. As only two megabytes are allocated to a RAM disk, the other one is free for use as a cache. If your machine is similarly configured, you can place the following command in AUTOEXEC.BAT

*Cache size*

```
c:\norton\ncache-f /ext=1000
```

to use the available memory. If, on the other hand, you are working on an XT computer with only 640K of conventional memory, you may want to have a cache of only 50K or so:

```
c:\norton\ncache-s /dos=50
```

Even with a cache this small, the improvement in performance will be noticeable.

Try adding a command appropriate to your configuration to your AUTOEXEC.BAT. The command should be added at the end of the file. When you have made the edit, reboot your computer. When the cache is loaded upon rebooting, you will see the Cache Status screen shown in Figure 20.1.

The amount of DOS, extended, and/or expanded memory dedicated to the cache is listed at the top of the screen. In Figure 20.1, for example, the cache takes up 9K of DOS memory and the software managing the cache takes up another 65K, leaving 473K for applications. In addition, one megabyte (1000K) of extended memory is dedicated to the cache, leaving 2328K free (for RAM disks, etc.).

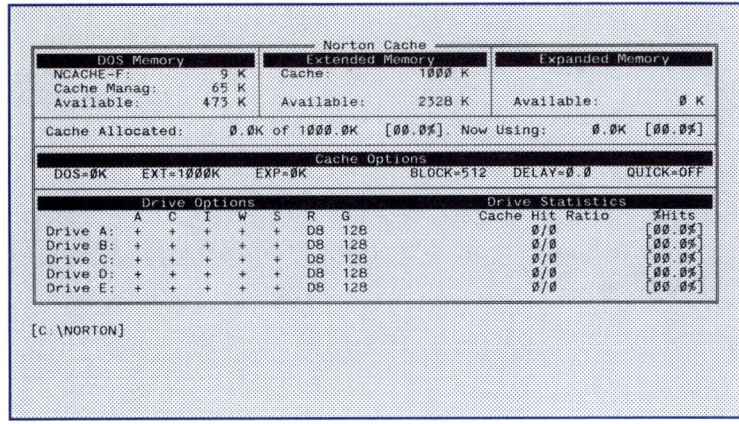

■ *Figure 20.1: The Cache Status screen*

The *Cache Allocated* prompt tells you how much of the cache contains data. In Figure 20.1, the cache is empty (0.0K of 1000.0K).

The *Cache Options* prompt repeats some information—namely, how much memory is dedicated to the cache. The other information on this screen is beyond the scope of this book.

## RECONFIGURING A CACHE

Having loaded a cache, you will probably notice the increase in speed right away. A situation might arise, however, where you need to change the size of a cache to free up some memory. To reconfigure a cache, you must first remove it from memory by entering the following at the command prompt:

```
ncache-f /uninstall
```

Try this now. You should get a message that the cache has been uninstalled.

Removing a cache from memory is possible only if the cache was the last TSR to be loaded. This is why you place the cache command at the end of your AUTOEXEC.BAT file.

Once the cache has been removed from memory, you can reload it, specifying its new size. Enter the NCACHE-F command at the command line just as you placed it in your AUTOEXEC.BAT file, but with different options specified. For example, to shrink the one megabyte cache mentioned above to a cache half its size, you would enter

```
c:\ncache-f /ext=500
```

Or, if the 50K DOS cache is too large:

```
c:\ncache-s /dos=30
```

The cache you load with this command will remain in effect for the duration of the current session (until you reboot your machine or reconfigure it again).

If you decide that you would like to work with a cache for a while, leave the cache command in your AUTOEXEC.BAT (or change it to some other more appropriate size). If you don't want to keep it, remove it now.

# Index

## A

ANSI.SYS driver, 129
archive files, 95
ASCII characters, 86–87
ASK command, 120–123
attributes
  file, 94–95
  screen, 24–25, 99–100, 128–130
AUTOEXEC.BAT files
  disk caching and, 150–153
  DISKMON program and, 72
  FILESAVE program and, 34
  IMAGE program and, 40
  path statement in, 7–8
  viewing contents of, 117

## B

background color, 99–100, 128–130
bad clusters, 42, 54, 57, 134
Batch Enhancer (BE) program. *See*
  batch files
batch files, 119–131
  creating a pause with, 126
  drawing boxes with, 125–126
  drawing windows with, 130–131
  positioning the cursor with,
    127–128
  repeating characters with, 126–127
  setting screen colors with, 128–130
  user-defined menus in, 120–123
  using sound in, 123–125
BEEP command, 123–125
bootable floppy disks, 52–53
border color, 99–100, 128–130
BOX command, 125–126
boxes, drawing with batch file,
  125–126

## C

CALIBRAT program, 133–140
clusters, bad, 42, 54, 57, 134
CMOS status, 115
colors, screen, 24–25, 99–100,
  128–130
CONFIG.SYS files
  data encryption and, 60
  device statements in, 116
  disk caching and, 150–153
  DISKREET program and, 60
  viewing contents of, 117
COUNTRY.SYS file, 103
CPU speed, 114, 116
cursor
  positioning of, 127–128
  size of, 99

## D

data encoding testing, 137–138
data encryption, 59–68
  CONFIG.SYS file and, 60
  file decryption, 63
  NDisks and, 59, 64–68
data files
  dBASE, 50
  Lotus 1-2-3, 48–49
  Symphony, 48–49
date set, 104
dBASE data files, 50
decryption, 63
defective disks, 42, 54, 57, 134
DELAY command, 126
delay time, key repetitions, 101–102
device drivers, 116
dialog box menus, 11–12

directories
  deleting, 108–109
  making, 108–109
  NCD program and, 105–109
  NORTON, 4
  renaming, 108–109
  root, 106
  sorting of files in, 146–148
  TRASHCAN, 32
  tree structure for, 105–107
disk caching, 149–154
  AUTOEXEC.BAT file and,
    150–153
  changing size of, 153–154
  CONFIG.SYS file and, 150–153
  fast caching, 150
  small caching, 149–150
disk configuration summary, 115
DISKEDIT (DE) program, 81–88
  FAT and, 83–85
  files and, 85–87
  unused clusters and, 87–88
DISKMON (Disk Monitor) program,
  69–73
  drive activity light and, 69, 72–73
  head parking utility and, 69, 73
  write-protecting disks with, 70–72
DISKREET program. See data
  encryption
disks. See floppy disks; hard disks
DISKTOOL program, 51–57
  bootable floppy disks and, 52–53
  defective disks and, 54–55
  DOS RECOVER program and, 57
  Mark as Cluster function and, 57
  rescue diskettes and, 55–57
DOS CD command, 107
DOS errorlevels, 122–123
DOS RECOVER program, 57
DOS SYS program, 52
drive activity light, 69, 72–73

E

erasing of disk data. See WIPEINFO
  program
errorlevels, 122–123
Esc key, 14–15

F

Fast Wipe, 80
File Allocation Table (FAT), 83–85
FILEFIND (FF) program, 89–95
  changing file attributes with, 94–95
  text searching with, 93–94
  viewing files with, 92–93
FILEFIX program, 47–50
files
  archive, 95
  ASCII code and, 86–87
  attributes of, 94–95
  changing attributes of, 94–95
  data. See data files
  decrypting, 63
  DISKEDIT program and, 85–87
  encrypting. See data encryption
  finding. See FILEFIND (FF)
    program
  fragmentation of, 141–146
  hexadecimal notation and, 85–86
  hidden, 77, 94
  read-only, 77, 94
  sorting within directories, 146–148
  system, 94
  unerasing, 27–32
  unfragmenting, 142–146
  wiping, 76–79
FILESAVE program, 32–34
floppy disks
  bootable, 52–53
  Norton Disk Doctor II and, 44–45
  rescue, 55–57

sector errors on, 54–55
wiping, 79–80
foreground color, 99–100, 128–130
FORMAT.EXE program,
   replacement of, 5
formatting, 5, 35–38
fragmentation of files, 141–146
full installation, 3
full-screen menus, 11–12

## G

Government Wipe, 80

## H

hard disks
  access time of, 136–137
  CALIBRAT program and, 133–140
  controller performance and,
    137–138
  data encoding testing on, 137–138
  file fragmentation on, 141–146
  with IDE controllers, 135
  interleave optimization of, 133–134,
    139–140
  low-level formatting of, 134
  parking heads on, 69, 73
  partitions on, 115–116
  pattern testing on, 134
  performance index of, 116
  with SCSI controllers, 135
  sector translation on, 135
  speed of, 114, 136–137, 142–148
  surface testing of, 42-n-44
  system integrity testing and, 136
  unfragmenting files on, 142–146
  wiping, 79–80
hardware interrupts, 115
hardware requirements, 1–2
head parking utility, 69, 73

hexadecimal notation, 85–86
hidden files, 77, 94

## I

IMAGE program, 35, 40
installation, 1–8
  configuration options, 5–8
  full, 3
  partial, 3
interleave optimization, 133–134,
    139–140

## K

keyboard
  dialog box menus and, 12
  full-screen menus and, 12
  lists and, 13–14
  pull-down menus and, 10
  repetition rate for, 101–102

## L

lists, 13–14
Lotus 1-2-3 data files, 48–49
low-level formatting, 134

## M

Mark as Cluster function, 57
memory block list, 116
memory-resident programs, 114
memory usage summary, 116
menus
  dialog box, 11–12
  full-screen, 11–12
  pull-down, 9–11
  user-defined, 120–123
mouse
  control options, 24–25
  dialog box menus and, 12

full-screen menus and, 12
lists and, 13–14
pull-down menus and, 10
radio buttons and, 12–13
speed of, 102
toggle options and, 12–13

## N

NCACHE-F program. *See* disk
   caching
NCACHE-S program. *See* disk
   caching
NDD. *See* Norton Disk Doctor
NDisks, 59, 64–68
   deleting, 68
   opening, 67
network configuration summary, 115
network performance summary, 116
Norton Change Directory (NCD)
   program, 105–109
Norton Control Center (NCC)
   program, 97–104
   changing color palette with, 100
   changing text colors with, 99–100
   changing video mode with, 100
   country information and, 103
   date/time setting in, 104
   keyboard sensitivity and, 101–102
   mouse sensitivity and, 102
   serial port configuration and, 103
   setting cursor size with, 99
   stopwatches in, 103
NORTON directory, 4
Norton Disk Doctor II (NDD), 41–45
   floppy disks and, 44–45
   surface testing and, 42–44
NORTON.EXE program, 9–10
Norton Utilities Shell, 17–25
   as a DOS shell, 21–23

modifying program list, 21–23
mouse control options, 24–25
sorting program listing in, 18–19
video mode options, 24–25

## P

palettes, 100
partial installation, 3
partition tables, 115–116
password control, 5–7
path statement, 7–8
pattern testing, 134
pause, creating with batch file, 126
ports, 103, 106–107
PRINTCHAR command, 126–127
printer ports, 106–107
prompts, 14
pull-down menus, 9–11

## R

radio buttons, 12–13
read-only files, 77, 94
recovery of disk data, 41–45, 47–57
repetition rate, keyboard, 101–102
rescue diskettes, 55–57
root directory, 106
ROWCOL command, 127–128

## S

SA (Screen Attributes) command,
   128–130
Safe Format program, 5, 35–38
screen colors, 24–25, 99–100,
   128–130
searching
   files, 90–92
   text, 93–94
sector errors, 54–55

sector translation, 135
serial ports, 103, 106–107
SFORMAT (Safe Format) program,
  5, 35–38
shortcut key combinations, 10–11
software interrupts, 115
sorting
  files within directories, 146–148
  NORTON program files, 18–19
speed of hard disk, 114, 136–137,
  142–148
SPEEDDISK program, 142–148
stopwatches, 103
surface testing, 42–44
Symphony data files, 48–49
SYSINFO program, 111–117
system files, 94
system information, 20–21, 111–117
system integrity testing, 136

## T

text, searching of, 93–94
time set, 104
toggle options, 12–13
TRASHCAN directory, 32

## U

UNERASE program, 27–32
UNFORMAT program, 35, 38–40
unfragmentation, 142–146
user-defined menus, 120–123
user interface, 9–15

## V

video configuration summary,
  114–115
video modes, 24–25, 100

## W

wildcard characters, 76
WINDOW command, 130–131
windows, drawing with batch file,
  130–131
WIPEINFO program, 75–80
  applied to disks, 79–80
  applied to files, 76–79
  configuring, 80
  wipe levels and, 80
write protection, 70–72